SIMPLE
ITALIAN
SNACKS

ALSO BY
JASON DENTON AND
KATHRYN KELLINGER

SIMPLE ITALIAN SANDWICHES
(WITH JENNIFER DENTON)

SIMPLE
ITALIAN
SNACKS

MORE RECIPES FROM AMERICA'S
FAVORITE PANINI BAR

JASON DENTON AND KATHRYN KELLINGER
PHOTOGRAPHY BY MICHAEL PIAZZA

WM
WILLIAM MORROW
An Imprint of HarperCollinsPublishers

HarperCollins books may be purchased for educational, business, or sales promotional use. For information please write: Special Markets Department, HarperCollins Publishers, 10 East 53rd Street, New York, NY 10022.

FIRST EDITION

Designed by Lorie Pagnozzi

Photographs by Michael Piazza

Library of Congress Cataloging-in-Publication Data

Denton, Jason.
    Simple Italian snacks : more recipes from America's favorite panini bar /
        Jason Denton and Kathryn Kellinger; photography by Michael Piazza. — 1st ed.
    p. cm.
    Includes index.
    ISBN 978-0-06-143508-9
    1. Snack foods. 2. Cookery, Italian. I. Kellinger, Kathryn. II. Title.

TX740.D4664 2008
641.5945—dc22   2008015741

08 09 10 11 12 WBC/RRD 10 9 8 7 6 5 4 3 2 1

*To my amazing wife, Jennifer, and my
two little dudes, Jack and Finn, I love you*

—Jason Denton

*For Kay and George and
all that took place in
the kitchen*

—Kathryn Kellinger

CONTENTS

INTRODUCTION

Breakfast, lunch, and dinner all have their merits—books have been written, families raised, and important business conducted over all of these meals. But for my family and me, most of our meals are built from snacks; delicious ingredients arranged into an assortment of small plates. Lively, fun, and sophisticated, these snacks are born from the union of the Italian tradition of antipasti and the modern American lifestyle. The pace at the table is leisurely, and the time spent in the kitchen is just as relaxed.

Small plates, bar snacks, antipasti, and tapas—these are familiar terms to most of the American restaurant-going public. Social and stylish, this type of cuisine is the basis for my weekends with friends and family, midweek nights at home with the neighbors, or just the kids on a Sunday morning. Like everybody else, I don't have the time to make elaborate meals—I save that for holidays. But we do a lot of entertaining all year long, and this is the food that makes it possible. Beside the ease of advance preparation, the prolonged nibbling of snacks and small plates is conducive to extended conversation and elongated lounging—both of which should be national pastimes.

The Italian custom of antipasti has gained popularity in restaurants recently (even though it existed in medieval times) with broad tables of small plates to entice the guests as they enter, offering something to nibble on while considering the rest of the meal. The food I serve at my restaurants—'ino, Lupa, 'inotecca, and Bar Milano—is made and served in the tradition of Italian conviviality. The dishes in this book have been road tested—these are the ones my friends love and look for when they arrive for a summer weekend or an afternoon of football.

The chapters in this book are based on occasions: time spent with friends and family and what you might serve them. Each chapter lists a selection of items that are especially suited to, say, having friends over, casual picnics, or serving a sit-down dinner. Seasons come into play mostly in spirit, but occasionally the fleeting availability of an ingredient like figs or corn dictates a snack that celebrates the season.

Panini, tramezzini, and bruschetta continue to be major players in our home entertaining. In *Simple Italian Sandwiches* I highlighted many of the classic combinations—the iconic sandwiches of Italy. I've added more here, but I've focused on regional combinations such as a panini of speck, cabbage, and poppy seeds (page 138), flavors that you might find in the northern Alpine region of Italy. Or I have featured what I consider an Italian approach to worldwide ingredients, like the Tramezzini of Duck Confit Salad with Pickled Squash Mayonnaise (page 100). This type of snacking continues to be inspiring—the combination of simplicity and endless possibilities is what *Simple Italian Snacks* hopes to embody.

Use the occasions as a starting point, and then compose your menus based on your own style and preferences. What all of these snacks share is a simplicity of preparation and an Italian approach toward ingredients. There are combinations that are authentic and others that I think channel the spirit of Italian cooking. This is food to have fun with—preparing it, serving it, and, of course, eating it. My travels and restaurants are where the ideas for these dishes are born, but my home and family are where they take shape, and where the table really comes alive. Cheers!

APERITIVO—DRINKS
WITH FRIENDS

INVITING FRIENDS OVER FOR DRINKS IS LIBERATING—THIS IS FREE-FORM socializing, unlike dinner parties with their tyrannical schedules of cooking times and seating charts. Guests should be able to reach for a bite to eat as easily as they might refill their glass. The host should be able to laugh and gossip with abandon, knowing that there's not much to do in the kitchen. The first recipe in this chapter, Shallow-Fried Brussels Sprouts, gives you an opportunity to hold court: you at the stove, your guests at the kitchen counter, chatting over a glass of Prosecco.

SHALLOW-FRIED BRUSSELS SPROUTS

TRAMEZZINI OF EGG WITH ITALIAN TUNA

'INO MAYONNAISE

BRUSCHETTA OF WHITE BEANS WITH EGG YOLK VINAIGRETTE AND TOMATO

TALEGGIO, APPLE, AND PISTACHIO PANINI

BRUSCHETTA OF HERBED RICOTTA AND BLACK PEPPER

MILANO MIXER

ALMOND ORANGE BISCOTTI

SHALLOW-FRIED BRUSSELS SPROUTS

Deep-fried flavor using only a minimum of oil—this is my at-home method of frying. With brussels sprouts, I pull the leaves from the globe and let them sizzle to a delicate crunch. Thin, crisp, and salty, they're a leafy green garden alternative to nuts and chips when serving cocktails. And people are always surprised to find that they *do* like brussels sprouts, at least when they're prepared this way.

SERVES 4

6 cups vegetable oil

1 pint brussels sprouts, leaves separated

Sea salt

4 slices prosciutto di Parma, cut into thin ribbons (optional)

1. Pour the vegetable oil into a large (10-inch) straight-sided sauté pan. Heat it over a medium-high flame until a brussels sprout leaf sizzles vigorously when dropped in.

2. Working in batches, add the leaves to the hot oil and fry them for 2 minutes, until they are crisp and golden. Using a slotted spoon, transfer them to a paper-towel-lined tray. Immediately sprinkle the fried leaves with sea salt. Let the oil reheat before adding another batch.

3. Let the leaves cool for 2 minutes before dividing them between two small serving dishes.

4. Scatter the prosciutto over the fried leaves, if using, before serving.

TRAMEZZINI OF EGG WITH ITALIAN TUNA

This sandwich is one of those so-basic-but-so-sophisticated combinations. Embodying the Italian love of simple ingredients, this tramezzino combines two kitchen staples: canned tuna and hard-boiled eggs. Use homemade mayonnaise, add a glass of Verdicchio, and the effect is pure luxury.

SERVES 4

8 ounces canned Italian tuna

$^1/_2$ cup Lemon Mayonnaise (page 8)

8 slices pullman bread (square sandwich loaf also called "pain de mie"; Arnold Brick Oven White is a fine substitute)

2 hard-boiled eggs (see below), sliced

Sea salt

Freshly ground black pepper

1. Drain the tuna and flake it with a fork in a mixing bowl. Add the Lemon Mayonnaise and combine. (If making fresh mayo isn't on your agenda, add the juice of 1 lemon to 2 tablespoons of Hellmann's, which is called Best Foods on the West Coast. Whisk to combine.)

2. Arrange half of the bread slices on a clean work surface. Spread a thin layer of tuna over each slice, covering it completely. Arrange the egg slices over the tuna, and then season with sea salt and freshly ground black pepper. Cover with the remaining bread slices and press gently.

3. Remove the crusts with a serrated knife, cut each sandwich in half diagonally, and serve.

HARD-BOILED EGGS Two techniques, based on personality type.

If you can watch water coming to a boil, here's the method for you: Place 2 eggs in a saucepan and cover with water. Place over a high flame, and when the water comes to a boil, remove the pan from the heat. Let the eggs sit in the water for 8 minutes. Drain, and rinse under cool water.

If you're easily distracted: Bring a pot of water to a boil. When you notice that it's boiling, reduce the heat to a bare simmer. Gently lower the eggs into the water and set a kitchen timer for 11 minutes. Drain, and rinse under cool water.

Both of these methods produce an egg with a firm white and a creamy yolk. Peel just before using. The eggs should *not* be refrigerated.

'INO MAYONNAISE

Homemade mayonnaise feels like a luxury until you realize that it's a necessity—you just can't go back to the jar after tasting the superior flavor of homemade.

5 large egg yolks

1½ tablespoons water

Juice of 1 lemon

2 teaspoons salt

1¾ cups olive oil

1. In a blender, using a slow speed, combine the egg yolks, water, lemon juice, and salt.

2. Partially cover the open blender with a towel to cut down on splatter, turn the blender up to high, and begin adding the olive oil in a slow and steady stream. Adding the olive oil should take 5 to 7 minutes. As the mayonnaise begins to thicken, the towel will no longer be necessary and the blender will be less noisy. Watch as the mayonnaise thickens, being careful to maintain the speed at which you add the olive oil.

3. Store the mayonnaise in the refrigerator in a bowl covered with plastic wrap or in a plastic tub with a tight-fitting lid for up to 4 days.

Save your best extra-virgin olive oil for another use. Mayonnaise calls for a mild oil with no pronounced taste, so the less expensive olive oils work best.

LEMON AND TRUFFLED MAYONNAISE

The mayonnaise can be flavored to suit its use: Replace ¼ cup of the olive oil with an equal amount of truffled olive oil for Truffled Mayonnaise. Add an additional tablespoon of lemon juice to give the mayo a more pronounced citrus flavor for Lemon Mayonnaise.

BRUSCHETTA OF WHITE BEANS WITH EGG YOLK VINAIGRETTE AND TOMATO

This is as fast and stylish as a Fiat. Freshly cooked white beans are the scenic long route; canned beans are the rush-hour shortcut. Both roads lead to a bruschetta of an egg-enriched vinaigrette over creamy white beans.

MAKES 8 BRUSCHETTA

2 hard-boiled eggs (see page 7), yolks minced with a fork, whites finely chopped

1 cup extra-virgin olive oil

2 cups cooked white beans, drained and rinsed

2 medium tomatoes, cored and cut into a medium dice

Grated zest of 1 lemon

Sea salt

Freshly ground black pepper

8 baguette slices, cut ½ inch thick on the diagonal, toasted

1. Combine the egg yolks with ¼ cup of the olive oil and whisk together. Put the beans and the tomatoes in a bowl, and pour the mixture over them. Add the chopped egg whites and the lemon zest. Toss gently to combine while adding the remaining ¾ cup olive oil. Season with sea salt and freshly ground black pepper.

2. Top each toast with a layer of white beans. Give each bruschetta a turn of a pepper mill before serving on a large platter.

TALEGGIO, APPLE, AND PISTACHIO PANINI

I think of this as a cheese board packed into a sandwich—there's the rich and runny cheese, the sweet and crisp apple, and the salty crunch of nuts. This is a great way to enjoy Taleggio, a full-flavored cow's milk cheese that melts into a silky tang.

MAKES 4 PANINI

1/2 cup shelled unsalted pistachio nuts

1/2 crisp, sweet apple, such as Macoun or Fuji, unpeeled, very thinly sliced

4 ciabatta rolls, domed tops sliced off, rolls sliced in half horizontally

8 ounces Taleggio, rind removed, at room temperature

Sea salt

Freshly ground black pepper

1. Preheat the oven to 250°F.

2. Spread the pistachios on a baking sheet and toast them in the oven until they are aromatic, 3 minutes. When they have cooled, roughly chop them.

3. Preheat a panini grill.

4. Arrange 4 apple slices on the bottom half of each ciabatta roll. Top with the sliced Taleggio. (This cheese will spread in the panini press, so don't go to the edge of the bread.) Top with 4 more apple slices and a sprinkling of toasted pistachios. Season with sea salt and freshly ground black pepper. Place the top half of the ciabatta on each sandwich.

5. Grill the sandwiches for 3 minutes, or until the cheese has melted and the bread is golden brown.

6. Slice each sandwich in half and serve immediately.

BRUSCHETTA OF HERBED RICOTTA AND BLACK PEPPER

This is a great example of the Simple Italian philosophy. Buy a little fresh ricotta, add some herbaceous olive oil, and with a few quick steps you've got something greater than the sum of its parts.

SERVES 4

½ cup olive oil

⅓ cup fresh basil leaves, packed

⅓ cup fresh oregano leaves, packed

⅓ cup fresh thyme leaves, packed

1 cup fresh ricotta

8 baguette slices, cut ½ inch thick on the diagonal, toasted

4 fresh basil leaves, cut into thin ribbons, for garnish

Sea salt

Freshly ground black pepper

1. In a small sauté pan, combine the olive oil and the fresh herbs. Heat over a low flame for 3 to 4 minutes, until the herbs become aromatic and the oil is infused with their flavor. Remove from the heat and strain the oil into a medium mixing bowl. Discard the herbs.

2. Add the fresh ricotta to the herb-infused oil and whisk until smooth.

3. Spoon 2 tablespoons of the herbed ricotta over each toasted baguette slice. Garnish with a few strands of fresh basil, a sprinkling of sea salt, and a half-turn of a pepper mill. Serve immediately.

MILANO MIXER

First make a simple syrup: Combine 1 cup fresh blood orange juice (6 oranges) with ¼ cup sugar in a small saucepan. Heat over a low flame until the sugar has entirely dissolved and the mixture is reduced by half, about 5 minutes. Store in a glass jar and keep for up to 1 week. For each drink, combine 1 ounce blood orange syrup, 1 ounce Campari, 4 ounces sparkling water, and a dash of bitters. Pour over ice, garnish with a blood orange slice, and serve.

ALMOND ORANGE BISCOTTI

These are a version of the classic twice-baked wine-dipping biscuit found all over Italy. With a firm bite, these biscuits are meant to be softened in an afternoon espresso or glass of Chianti. They become kid-friendly when dunked in Chocolate Espresso Fondue (page 51), but these are very much cookies for grown-ups.

The biscotti will keep for several days in an airtight tin or cookie jar and are wonderful to take along to a dinner party.

MAKES 2 DOZEN BISCOTTI

1½ cups blanched almonds

2 cups all-purpose flour

1 cup sugar

1 teaspoon baking soda

¼ teaspoon salt

2 large eggs, at room temperature, plus 1 additional, lightly beaten, for brushing over the shaped dough

1 egg yolk, at room temperature

1 teaspoon vanilla extract

Grated zest of 1 orange

1. Preheat the oven to 325°F.

2. Spread the almonds on a baking sheet and toast them in the oven until they are aromatic, 3 minutes. When they have cooled, roughly chop them. Leave the oven on.

3. In the work bowl of a food processor, combine the flour, sugar, baking soda, and salt. Pulse to combine.

4. In a large spouted measuring cup, whisk together 2 of the eggs, egg yolk, vanilla, and orange zest. With the food processor running, pour the egg mixture down the feed tube, processing only until the ingredients begin to come together. Turn off the machine, add half of the almonds, and pulse 5 times. Add the rest of the almonds, and pulse 5 more times.

5. Transfer the dough to a floured board and shape it into 2 logs, each about 2½ inches in diameter. Place them on a parchment-lined baking sheet, with a few inches of space between them, and brush them with the remaining, beaten egg.

6. Bake for 30 minutes, or until the tops are golden and feel firm to the touch. Remove the baking sheet from the oven and set it aside until the logs are cool enough to handle, 15 minutes or so.

7. Cut the logs on the diagonal, into slices that are about ¾ inch thick. Lay the slices flat on the baking sheet and return it to the oven. Bake for 10 minutes on each side for a golden crisp texture.

NEW YEAR'S DAY

THE PARTY AFTER THE PARTY, NEW YEAR'S DAY IS A MORNING- after menu for those occasions when you want the good times to continue. Partying to the wee hours is exhausting, so the next day's brunch should be substantial enough to bring everyone back to life. This menu offers choices for an easy but stylish buffet of hearty cold-weather food that can be served throughout the day—from brunch to early supper. Serve strong coffee and wear your best robe. Postpone resolutions if possible.

LENTIL BRUSCHETTA WITH FRIED EGG

WARM SALAD OF BUTTERNUT SQUASH

EGGS BAKED IN TOMATO SAUCE

STEAK SPIEDINI WITH CHERRY TOMATOES AND 'INO PESTO

SWEET FENNEL SAUSAGE PANINI

BLOODY BRANCA

BRUSCHETTA OF RICOTTA, ANCHOVY, AND CHERRY TOMATO

AFFOGATO

LENTIL BRUSCHETTA WITH FRIED EGG

A traditional Italian New Year's Eve dinner includes cotechino sausage and lentils to ensure good fortune for the year ahead. A traditional New Year's Day in New York might include a hangover and a hearty brunch that sends everyone back to bed for an afternoon nap. This small but filling dish fits the bill perfectly, and includes the lucky lentils if not the sausage. It's incredibly delicious and easy to make.

SERVES 4

2 tablespoons butter

3 leeks, white parts only, split, thinly sliced, and rinsed

1 teaspoon salt

1 cup red or rosé wine

1 cup dried lentils

2 cups water

Extra-virgin olive oil

1 teaspoon red wine vinegar

4 baguette slices, cut ½ inch thick on the diagonal, toasted

4 extra-large eggs

Sea salt

Freshly ground black pepper

1. Melt the butter in a medium saucepan over a medium-high flame. When the foam subsides, add the leeks and the salt. Cook, stirring frequently, until the leeks are soft and translucent but haven't taken on any color, about 5 minutes. Add the wine and let it bubble away until the pan is almost dry, 5 to 7 minutes.

2. Add the lentils and use a wooden spatula to move them around in the pan for a minute or two. Then add the water and bring it to a boil over a high flame. Reduce the heat to a simmer, cover, and cook until the water has been absorbed, 15 minutes. Remove the pan from the heat, add 1 teaspoon olive oil and the red wine vinegar, and stir to combine. Cover to keep the lentils warm while you fry the eggs.

3. Place the baguette slices on serving plates next to the stove.

4. Heat 2 tablespoons olive oil in a 9-inch nonstick pan over a medium-high flame. Swirl the pan to coat the bottom, and when the oil shimmers, crack 2 eggs into the pan. Cook for 2 to 3 minutes, until the edges are brown and the yolk has set. Top 2 toasts with ½ cup of the lentils, and then use a slotted spatula to top each with a fried egg. Fry the remaining 2 eggs and assemble the remaining bruschetta. Sprinkle each with sea salt and a generous amount of freshly ground black pepper. Serve immediately.

WARM SALAD OF BUTTERNUT SQUASH

Escarole is a slightly bitter green often found in rustic soups. As a salad green, it offers a lovely crispness and a pretty pale color, and it's an attractive backdrop for other similarly strong ingredients. Its smooth bitterness is combined best with something naturally sweet and decidedly salty. Caperberries, the fruits that form if capers are left on the plant, add a distinctive salinity and texture to the dish. This vibrant salad can start off a meal or be a main course on its own.

SERVES 4

3 tablespoons olive oil

2½ tablespoons honey

3 cups diced butternut squash (½-inch pieces)

8 caperberries, stemmed and quartered

½ head radicchio, cut into ½-inch strips

½ cup dried currants

1 head escarole, stem end removed, dark outer tips of the leaves trimmed away

1 tablespoon sherry vinegar

6 slices prosciutto di Parma, sliced into 1½-inch-long ribbons

Sea salt

Freshly ground black pepper

1. Combine the olive oil and the honey in a large straight-sided sauté pan. Add the squash and toss to coat.

2. Place the pan over medium-high heat and cook, stirring occasionally, until the squash is tender and lightly browned on the edges, 8 to 10 minutes. Add the caperberries, radicchio, and currants to the pan and stir to combine. Continue to cook a minute more to slightly wilt the radicchio. Remove from the heat. (These ingredients can be served warm or at room temperature.)

3. Just before serving, add the escarole and the sherry vinegar. Toss well and divide among four serving plates. Top each serving with a few ribbons of prosciutto, a sprinkling of sea salt, and a few turns of a pepper mill.

CURRANTS The zante currant is a dried seedless grape, brighter in color and sweeter in taste than raisins; raisins or chopped dried prunes can be used as substitutes here.

EGGS BAKED IN
TOMATO SAUCE

From celebratory Easter breads to egg pasta, eggs are central to every-day Italian life from morning 'til night. Like a frittata, this humble egg dish satisfies around the clock and makes the best use of ingredients that you've probably got on hand. Supremely filling and satisfying, this soothing dish can be served with a morning coffee or an evening glass of Pigato, a slightly obscure Ligurian wine—its medium body and nice acid would be the perfect companion.

The tomato sauce can be made the day before and reheated before as-sembling the dish, or bottled sauce can stand in its place. The Milk-Soaked Croutons add a bread-pudding-like texture and are well worth the ad-vance planning (they too can be made the day before or even earlier—you can store them in an airtight container for up to 4 days). Cook the eggs in individual ramekins or mini cast-iron pans, or cook them all to-gether in a 9-inch skillet and then ladle them into individual bowls.

SERVES 4

One 28-ounce can whole tomatoes

1½ teaspoons salt

1 teaspoon dried oregano

1 teaspoon grated lemon zest

¼ teaspoon red pepper flakes

1 teaspoon extra-virgin olive oil

1 teaspoon red wine vinegar

2 cups Milk-Soaked Croutons (page 59)

4 eggs

4 ounces Italian fontina cheese, sliced

1. Pour the tomatoes, along with their juice, into a medium saucepan. Using a knife or kitchen shears, break them down to small bite-size pieces. Add the salt, oregano, lemon zest, red pepper flakes, olive oil, and vinegar. Stir to combine, and bring to a gentle simmer over a medium flame. Cook for 45 minutes, or until the sauce has re-duced down to about 2 cups. Keep warm.

2. Preheat the broiler and set the broiling pan in the middle.

3. If you are using individual ramekins, cover the bottoms with a layer of Milk-Soaked Croutons, making them high-est around the edges, creating a "nest." Divide the warm tomato sauce among the ramekins, again creating a little indentation in the center. Crack an egg into each nest, and arrange the sliced fontina around the eggs.

If you are using one ovenproof skillet, line it with a layer of Milk-Soaked Croutons, followed by the

½ cup fresh arugula, roughly chopped

Sea salt

Freshly ground black pepper

sauce. Crack each of the eggs into the skillet so they orbit the center. Lay the fontina over the eggs.

4. Broil until the yolks are set but still runny and the cheese has melted, 4 to 6 minutes. Garnish each egg with a sprinkling of chopped arugula, sea salt, and freshly ground black pepper. Serve immediately.

STEAK SPIEDINI WITH CHERRY TOMATOES AND 'INO PESTO

Bites of grilled steak, bursts of cherry tomatoes, and the spirit-lifting power of pesto make this a favorite year-round snack. Serve it over a bed of arugula for a complete little dinner.

You'll need six bamboo skewers soaked in water to prevent burning, or metal ones.

SERVES 6

1 sirloin steak, about 1¼ pounds, cut into 1-inch cubes (18 pieces)

24 cherry tomatoes

½ cup extra-virgin olive oil

Sea salt

Freshly ground black pepper

1 cup 'Ino Pesto (page 69)

1. Combine the cubes of steak and the cherry tomatoes in a large bowl. Add the olive oil, toss to coat the ingredients, and let marinate for at least 1 hour and up to 8.

2. Preheat an outdoor grill or the broiler.

3. Thread the cherry tomatoes and the steak cubes onto 6 skewers, 4 tomatoes and 3 steak cubes on each. Season the skewers with sea salt and freshly ground black pepper.

4. If you are using an outdoor grill, cook the skewers over high heat with the lid closed for 6 to 8 minutes, turning the skewers halfway through. If using charcoal, cook the skewers over indirect heat to prevent flame flare-ups. If you are using the broiler, cook the skewers for 3 minutes per side for medium-rare, or 4 minutes per side for medium.

5. Place the skewers on a serving platter and spoon the 'Ino Pesto over each one, making a long, thin trail.

SWEET FENNEL SAUSAGE PANINI

This is a perfect reason to get to know your local Italian butcher: a standout snack that goes from good to great when you use fresh hand-made sausage.

·SERVES 4

4 sweet fennel sausages (about 4 ounces each)

4 ciabatta rolls, domed tops sliced off, rolls sliced in half horizontally

Fennel Mustard (recipe follows)

1 cup roughly chopped arugula

6 ounces Italian fontina cheese, sliced

1. Preheat the oven to 400°F.

2. Place the sausages in a small baking dish and bake for 25 minutes. Remove from the oven and let cool to room temperature.

3. Preheat a panini grill to high.

4. Spread the bottom half of each ciabatta roll with a thin layer of Fennel Mustard. Cut each sausage on the diagonal into 1-inch-thick slices, and arrange the slices in a single layer on the mustard-coated rolls. Top each with $1/4$ cup chopped arugula and then the fontina slices. The cheese should cover the sausage and arugula entirely, with no overhang. Cover each sandwich with the top half of the ciabatta.

5. Grill the sandwiches until the bread is golden brown and the cheese is set, about 4 minutes. Cut into triangles and serve immediately.

BLOODY BRANCA

This take on the Bloody Mary features Fernet Branca, an *amaro*, or bitter digestive, made with forty herbs and spices. This makes 4 drinks: Combine 6 ounces vodka, 12 ounces tomato juice, the juice of $\frac{1}{2}$ lemon, the juice of $\frac{1}{2}$ lime, a pinch of sea salt, freshly ground black pepper to taste, $\frac{1}{2}$ ounce Fernet Branca, and a dash of Worcestershire sauce in a shaker or pitcher. Shake or stir with ice and strain into chilled martini glasses. For a surprising spicy crunch, garnish each drink with a pickled red pepper sliver (page 151).

FENNEL MUSTARD

This recipe calls for *vincotto* (literally "cooked wine") vinegar, made in Apulia. The vinegar is dark and deeply flavored; substitute balsamic (which has a woodier taste) if you don't have *vincotto*.

MAKES $\frac{1}{2}$ CUP

2 fennel bulbs, cored and diced (2 cups)

3 tablespoons extra-virgin olive oil

1 teaspoon salt

Freshly ground black pepper

2 tablespoons honey

2 tablespoons *vincotto* vinegar

2 tablespoons sparkling water

$1\frac{1}{2}$ teaspoon dry mustard

1. Preheat the oven to 400°F.

2. Spread the diced fennel out on a foil-lined baking sheet, and drizzle the olive oil over it. Sprinkle with the salt and pepper to taste. Bake until the fennel is soft and molten, 20 to 25 minutes. Let cool to room temperature.

3. In a blender, combine the cooked fennel, the honey, *vincotto*, sparkling water, and dry mustard. Blend until nearly smooth. The mustard can be kept refrigerated in an airtight container for up to 3 days.

BRUSCHETTA OF RICOTTA, ANCHOVY, AND CHERRY TOMATO

Not the anchovies you think you know but marinated white anchovies. Packed in oil rather than salt, these are mild tasting with just the perfect amount of salinity. Their silky texture is another reason to love these delicious little fish.

SERVES 4

2 tablespoons extra-virgin olive oil, plus more for drizzling over the bruschetta

½ pint cherry tomatoes (16 to 18 tomatoes)

Salt

Freshly ground black pepper

8 baguette slices, cut ½ inch thick on the diagonal, toasted

1 cup ricotta

4 ounces marinated white anchovies

1. Heat the olive oil in a medium nonstick pan over a medium-high flame. Add the cherry tomatoes and season with salt and freshly ground black pepper to taste. Cook the tomatoes until they begin to crack and char, about 3 minutes. Transfer to a bowl to cool. When the tomatoes are cool enough to handle, press each with your finger to flatten slightly and prevent messy bursting when they are being eaten.

2. Spread each toast with fresh ricotta, covering the toast completely. Top each toast with 2 cherry tomatoes and then 2 white anchovy fillets. Coarsely grind black pepper over each bruschetta and serve.

AFFOGATO (ICE CREAM AND ESPRESSO)

Not quite a full-fledged dessert, *affogato* is a little something to end the meal on an up note. Serve this in small bowls or in coffee cups, and if you're in love with java, double the shots of espresso. If you don't have an espresso machine, buy take-out shots to bring home and microwave just before pouring over the ice cream.

SERVES 4

1 cup vanilla
ice cream

4 shots espresso
(approximately 8 ounces total),
piping hot

Semisweet chocolate for
grating over the top (optional)

1. Divide the ice cream among four ceramic cups or tumblers.

2. Pour ¼ cup of hot espresso into each cup. Grate chocolate over each, if using, and serve immediately.

If you own a handheld immersion whisk designed especially for milk, heat 2 tablespoons of milk in each coffee cup first and whisk each to a froth. Pour the espresso through the frothy milk and then add the ice cream. This makes a creamier, coffee milk-shake-type dessert.

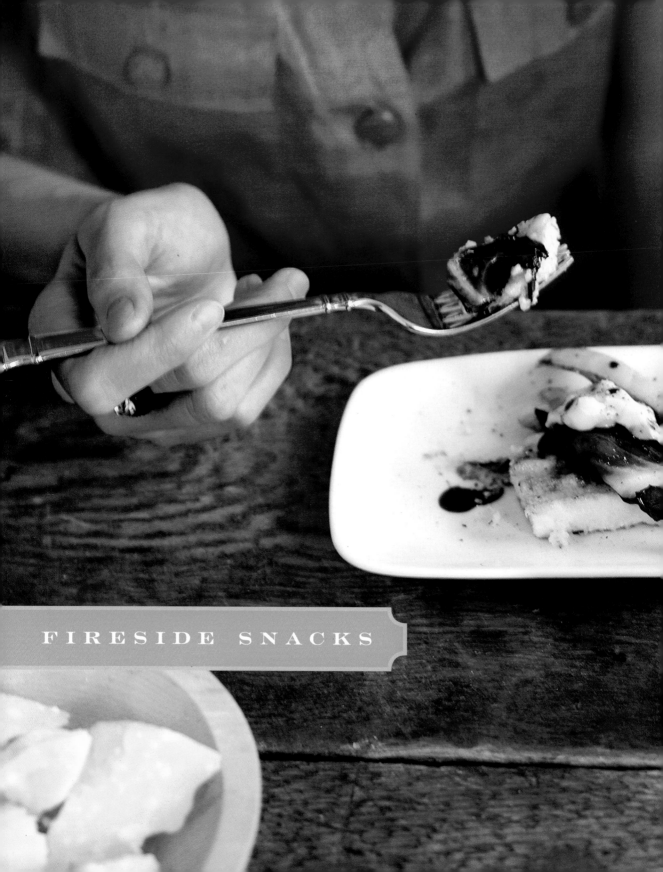

FIRESIDE SNACKS

THE BEST PART OF WINTER IS THE SANCTIONED LAZY AFTER-noon. It's too cold to go out, and there's not a lot of drive to do anything more than eat, drink, and play Scrabble. Earthy ingredients and hearty, rich flavors create coziness on an otherwise icy day. These are dishes that settle in nicely next to a game board, or on a coffee table to be reached from the couch. Good wine and a nap complete the picture.

RED BEET SALAD WITH
PISTACHIOS

BRESAOLA WITH RADICCHIO,
ARUGULA, CURRANTS,
AND CROTONESE

GRILLED POLENTA WITH BRAISED
RADICCHIO AND GORGONZOLA DOLCE

BRUSCHETTA OF WILTED BITTER
GREENS AND RICOTTA SALATA

PENNE, PEAS, AND PECORINO
FRITTATA

CABBAGE AND PANCETTA
BRUSCHETTA

SPIEDINI OF MEATBALLS, ONION, AND
SAGE

RED BEET SALAD
WITH PISTACHIOS

Alive with color, this salad combines earthy flavors with the vibrant colors of red beets and bright blood oranges. It's undeniably good for you and definitely delicious. On salad plates it's a great first course; on a large serving platter it's a gorgeous addition to an array of antipasti.

Use the tops of the beets for Roasted Beet Green Gratin (page 170) tomorrow.

SERVES 4

½ cup shelled unsalted pistachios

4 medium red beets, well rinsed, tops cut off

4 teaspoons plus ¼ cup extra-virgin olive oil

Sea salt

Freshly ground black pepper

2 blood oranges, cut into segments over a bowl, juice reserved

4 cups arugula, loosely packed, rinsed and spun dry

¼ cup red wine vinegar

Chunk of Pecorino Romano

1. Preheat the oven to 250°F.

2. Spread the pistachios on a baking sheet and toast them in the oven until they are lightly colored and fragrant, about 4 minutes, shaking the pan midway through. Set aside to cool.

3. Raise the oven temperature to 400°F.

4. Rub each beet with a teaspoon of olive oil. Place each beet on a square of aluminum foil, season with sea salt and freshly ground black pepper, and then wrap it up in the foil. Place them on a baking sheet and bake until tender, about 40 minutes. (The tip of a knife should easily pierce the beet.) Remove from the oven, unwrap, and let cool.

5. When the beets are cool enough to handle, peel them and cut them into ½-inch dice. In a medium mixing bowl, combine the diced beets, the orange segments, and the arugula.

6. Make a vinaigrette by combining the orange juice with the red wine vinegar and the ¼ cup olive oil. Dress the salad and toss gently. Season with sea salt and freshly ground black pepper to taste.

7. Divide the salad among four serving bowls. Sprinkle the salads with the toasted pistachio nuts and a generous grating of Pecorino Romano before serving.

BRESAOLA WITH RADICCHIO, ARUGULA, CURRANTS, AND CROTONESE

This is an elegant and rustic salad with a pronounced personality. Bresaola—air-dried paper-thin slices of beef—provides a salty, meaty base for the rest of the colorful ingredients. While this composed salad certainly looks elegant on a plate, in the most casual of situations, I recommend rolling the salad into the sliced bresaola (a roll-up) and eating it with your hands.

SERVES 4

1 head radicchio, shredded

1 cup arugula leaves

1 cup dried currants

1 tablespoon *aceto balsamico* (see page 36)

2 tablespoons extra-virgin olive oil

Juice of 1 lemon (about 2 tablespoons)

20 slices bresaola

Sea salt

Freshly ground black pepper

8 ounces Crotonese cheese, thinly sliced

1. Combine the shredded radicchio, arugula, and the currants in a small mixing bowl, and toss to combine. Combine the *aceto balsamico*, olive oil, and lemon juice in a small cup, and mix with a fork.

2. Arrange the slices of bresaola on four serving plates. Dress the salad with the olive oil mixture, season with sea salt and freshly ground black pepper, and then toss to combine. Place a handful of dressed salad in the center of each plate. Top each with the sliced Crotonese and a sprinkling of sea salt and freshly ground black pepper.

Crotonese is a firm sheep's milk cheese. Aged for a short period in wicker baskets, it has a mild but earthy flavor. If you can't locate Crotonese, a Pecorino Romano will work nicely.

GRILLED POLENTA WITH BRAISED RADICCHIO AND GORGONZOLA DOLCE

Grilled polenta, like toasts, can be the base for bruschetta or crostini. In its creamy state, polenta is served in the same way potatoes or noodles might be—as a backdrop for roasted meats. Grilling polenta amplifies its roasted corn flavor, perfect with the assertive combination of radicchio and Gorgonzola. Gorgonzola dolce is sweeter than the non-dolce variety, but most important, it's creamier and more luxurious. Eaten with a fork, this plate makes a fabulous first course.

The polenta should be made the day before and refrigerated overnight.

MAKES 12 SQUARES

¼ cup olive oil, plus extra for grilling

Firm Polenta (recipe follows)

1 head radicchio, cored, leaves separated

Salt

Freshly ground black pepper

8 ounces Gorgonzola dolce, crumbled

Aceto balsamico, (see page 36) for drizzling

1. Preheat a grill or a panini press.

2. If you are using a grill, brush the hot grill rack with olive oil. Brush olive oil over both sides of the polenta squares, and grill until they are warm and show grill marks, 4 to 5 minutes. Use a spatula to transfer the polenta to a serving platter.

   If you are using a panini press, brush olive oil over both sides of the polenta squares and the stationary part of the grill. Grill them on the press, without closing it, until they are warm and lightly browned, 4 to 5 minutes. Use a spatula to transfer the polenta to a serving platter.

3. Heat the ¼ cup olive oil in a sauté pan over a medium-high flame. Add the radicchio leaves and toss with tongs to coat the leaves with the oil. Cook until the radicchio has softened and the color has brightened, 4 minutes. Remove from the heat and season with salt and freshly ground black pepper.

4. Top each grilled polenta square with 2 pieces of wilted radicchio. Sprinkle crumbled Gorgonzola over each. Drizzle with *aceto balsamico,* and serve immediately.

ACETO BALSAMICO TRADIZIONALE DI MODENA Aged balsamic vinegar, made in Modena and left to condense down to an intense flavor and texture over the course of years, is a luxury that can easily be justified. A drop here, a drizzle there—a bottle of *aceto balsamico* will last, taking you through radicchio-topped polenta squares, dishes of fresh strawberries (their sweetness intensified with a few drops of this aged vinegar), or Bresaola with Radicchio, Arugula, Currants, and Crotonese (page 32), when every ingredient should be perfection. Keep your bottle of true Modena balsamic just behind your supermarket balsamic, and reach for it when balsamic vinegar has a small but starring role.

3. Add the polenta in a slow, steady stream, stirring it constantly with a wooden spoon in a slow figure-eight motion. Like pudding, the mixture will begin to thicken. Stir it every 2 minutes or so until all the liquid has been absorbed. Taste the polenta; it should be smooth and not at all grainy. Add a few tablespoons of water, up to $1/2$ cup, if all the liquid has been absorbed but the polenta still feels granular on the tongue, and continue cooking until all the liquid has been absorbed, 20 to 30 minutes.

4. Stir in the thyme leaves, and add salt to taste.

5. Pour the polenta into the prepared baking dish. Cover it with plastic wrap and refrigerate until firm, about 2 hours, or leave it overnight.

6. Cut the firm polenta into 3-inch squares and lift them out with a spatula. The squares can be fried in a nonstick pan or grilled on the bottom grill of a panini press until golden brown.

Firm polenta can be cut into sticks, fried in a little olive oil, dusted with grated Parmigiano-Reggiano, and served in a salad. It's a delicious textural counterpoint to leafy greens.

BRUSCHETTA OF WILTED BITTER GREENS AND RICOTTA SALATA

This is a great vehicle for salad greens that have lost their looks: wilt them down to their most flavorful, spread them on toasts, and suddenly your bruised arugula and watercress have found new life. The flavor is sophisticated, with ricotta salata lending a salty coolness to the bitter flavor of the greens. The ingredients are in your crisper drawer for this, one of my budget favorites.

MAKES 8 BRUSCHETTA

4 cups tightly packed bitter greens (arugula, watercress, radicchio, or a combination)

8 teaspoons olive oil

Sea salt

8 garlic cloves, crushed

2 tablespoons extra-virgin olive oil

8 baguette slices, cut ½ inch thick on the diagonal, toasted

4 ounces ricotta salata

1. Preheat the oven to 400°F.

2. Place the greens on a large rimmed baking sheet, arranging them in 8 small handfuls. Drizzle a teaspoon of olive oil over each handful, add a sprinkling of sea salt, and top with a crushed garlic clove.

3. Place the baking sheet in the oven and bake for 10 minutes, fluffing each handful of greens after 5 minutes.

4. Scoop the greens into a mixing bowl and let them cool to room temperature, then use tongs to transfer the greens to a cutting board, leaving any liquid behind. Roughly chop the greens and transfer them to a clean bowl. Drizzle with the extra-virgin olive oil.

5. Spread a tablespoon of the wilted greens over each toast. Top with a grating of ricotta salata and a light sprinkling of sea salt. Serve the toasts on a platter.

PENNE, PEAS, AND PECORINO FRITTATA

One of the greatest Italian snacks, a frittata can be served hot out of the pan or at room temperature. This long-life quality makes it perfect for an antipasti table or a buffet. As the ideal default dinner, a frittata is what to make when there's not much in the house. This one uses frozen organic peas for color and a little leftover penne, either in sauce or plain.

SERVES 4 TO 6

8 large eggs

1/2 cup milk

Salt

Freshly ground black pepper

1/2 cup grated Pecorino Romano

2 tablespoons butter

1 1/2 cups cooked penne

1/2 cup frozen peas, thawed

Extra-virgin olive oil

1. Preheat the broiler.

2. Whisk the eggs, milk, 1 teaspoon salt, 1 teaspoon pepper, and half of the grated Pecorino together in a medium bowl.

3. Heat a 9-inch nonstick pan with an ovenproof handle over a medium flame. Add the butter, tilting the pan to coat it well. Add the penne and the peas. Season with salt and freshly ground black pepper, then toss to coat the pasta and peas with the butter. Cook until they are heated through, 3 to 4 minutes. Spread the pasta and peas evenly over the bottom of the pan.

4. Raise the heat under the pan to medium-high. Add the egg mixture and cook, undisturbed, until the edges begin to thicken and set, about 2 minutes. Then use a rubber spatula to lift the edges toward the center of the pan, while tilting the pan so that the still-liquid egg mixture runs underneath. Continue cooking until the eggs are set but still moist on top. Sprinkle the remaining grated Pecorino over the frittata, and slide the pan under the broiler. Cook until the top of the frittata is golden and puffy, 4 to 5 minutes.

5. Let the pan cool for 5 minutes before sliding the frittata onto a serving plate (tilt the pan and use a spatula to slide it out). Drizzle the top with a fragrant extra-virgin olive oil, a sprinkling of salt, and some freshly ground black pepper. Cut into wedges and serve.

CABBAGE AND PANCETTA BRUSCHETTA

Besides being a hearty topping for toasts, this rustic combination can be tossed with cooked spaghetti for a peasant-style pasta dish. It's a blend of just a couple of humble ingredients that is disarmingly delicious.

MAKES 8 BRUSCHETTA

4 ounces pancetta, cut into matchsticks

½ head savoy cabbage, cored, sliced into thin ribbons

2 tablespoons plus 1 teaspoon red wine vinegar

1 teaspoon extra-virgin olive oil

8 baguette slices, cut ½ inch thick on the diagonal, toasted

Freshly ground black pepper

1. Preheat the oven to 400°F.

2. Spread the pancetta over a rimmed baking sheet, and scatter the sliced cabbage over the pancetta. Bake for 30 minutes, or until the cabbage is wilted and the pancetta is cooked but not crisp. Remove from the oven and drizzle the 2 tablespoons red wine vinegar over the cabbage. Toss the cabbage and pancetta to combine and to coat the cabbage with the rendered fat. Return the baking sheet to the oven and cook for 10 minutes more.

3. Remove the baking sheet from the oven and let the cabbage mixture cool for 10 minutes. Drizzle the olive oil over the cabbage mixture, along with the remaining 1 teaspoon red wine vinegar. Toss to combine.

4. Spoon a tablespoon of the cabbage mixture over each toast, and place the toasts on a serving platter. Top each bruschetta with freshly ground black pepper. Serve while the cabbage is still warm.

SPIEDINI OF MEATBALLS, ONION, AND SAGE

Spiedini, or skewers, offer a convenient way to cook and then serve all kinds of ingredients. These *spiedini*, with their precise squares of onion and sage, appeal to my design-driven friends. Good-looking and easy, they are perfect with a salad of mixed greens for a light meal or alongside cooked pasta for a deconstructed spaghetti and meatballs. My favorite way to serve them is a few on a platter, with slices of fresh bread and a little 'Ino Pesto (page 69). If you are using bamboo skewers, don't forget to soak them first in water for about 10 minutes to prevent burning.

MAKES 6 *SPIEDINI*

¾ cup fresh bread crumbs (from 2 slices of bread)

½ cup milk

½ small yellow onion, minced

1 garlic clove, minced

2 tablespoons chopped fresh parsley

2 tablespoons finely grated Parmigiano-Reggiano

8 ounces ground beef

8 ounces ground pork

1 large egg, lightly beaten

½ teaspoon salt

½ teaspoon black pepper

½ large yellow onion, cut into ½-inch squares

6 dried bay leaves, each cut into ½-inch squares

¼ cup olive oil

1. Combine the bread crumbs and the milk in a large bowl. Stir with a fork and let sit for 10 minutes to soften.

2. Add the minced onion, garlic, parsley, and Parmigiano-Reggiano to the bread-crumb mixture, and stir with a fork to combine. Add the meat, the beaten egg, and the salt and pepper. Use a fork at first to combine, then use your hands until the mixture is well blended. Roll into eighteen 1-inch meatballs. Transfer them to a paper-towel-lined tray. (The meatballs can be refrigerated at this point for up to 1 day.)

3. Preheat a grill or the broiler to high heat.

4. To make the *spiedini*, thread a meatball, followed by a square of onion and a square of bay leaf, onto a skewer. Continue alternating to make 6 skewers with 3 meatballs each. Lightly coat each with olive oil. Grill or broil the skewers for a total of 8 minutes, turning them halfway through.

SKI SNACKS

FOR MANY OF US, THE IDEAL COMING-IN-FROM-THE-COLD scenario involves the aroma of hearty food emanating from the kitchen. Bacon, cheese, warm spices, and melted chocolate all play a big role in this chapter. This is food for wintertime tapas-style dining. Serve it as an ongoing meal, a parade of snacks from late afternoon until evening. A long stretch of eating, drinking, and warming up by the fire is, I suspect, the whole point of skiing to begin with.

EGG YOLK PANCAKE WITH CAPERS

PORTOBELLO AND PANCETTA BRUSCHETTA

PANINI OF SMOKED MOZZARELLA, RADICCHIO, AND BALSAMICO

APICIAN SPICED CIDER

SPIEDINI OF PORK AND FENNEL

CHEESE PLATE WITH APPLE CONSERVA

CHOCOLATE ESPRESSO FONDUE

EGG YOLK PANCAKE WITH CAPERS

This is inspired by the *frittatina*, a small, thin omelette that's sliced into strips. My version uses yolks only. Not only is it rich and flavorful, it's the perfect use for leftovers when a guest demands an egg-whites-only breakfast. Whip this up for unexpected drop-ins and serve it while your guests open the wine.

The omission of salt is intentional, with all of the salinity coming from the capers.

MAKES 4 TO 6 APPETIZER PORTIONS

6 egg yolks

¼ cup milk

20 to 30 capers

1 teaspoon butter

1 teaspoon olive oil

2 tablespoons tomato paste

½ small yellow onion, thinly sliced

1. Beat the egg yolks lightly with a fork. Add the milk and the capers, and stir to combine.

2. Heat an 8-inch nonstick pan over a medium-high flame until you can feel the heat when you hold your hand above it.

3. Add the butter and the olive oil to the pan, and swirl to coat the bottom as the butter melts. Add the egg mixture and allow it to cook, undisturbed, for 3 minutes. Then flip the pancake with a spatula and cook the other side for just 1 minute (it shouldn't brown). Slide the pancake onto a cutting board. Spread the tomato paste over the top, and allow it to soak in for a moment or two.

4. Slice the pancake into wedges and top with the onion slices. Serve immediately.

PORTOBELLO AND PANCETTA BRUSCHETTA

In homage to my grandmother, who used to cook leftover Easter ham in condensed milk, this bruschetta combines the salty flavor of pork and the creamy sweetness of milk. If you have some leftover ham in the house, use it!

SERVES 4

4 ounces pancetta, diced

2 portobello mushroom caps, wiped clean with a damp paper towel and diced

¼ red onion, diced

¼ cup milk

1 teaspoon fresh thyme leaves

1 teaspoon fresh lemon juice

Salt

Freshly ground black pepper

8 baguette slices, cut ½ inch thick on the diagonal, toasted

1. Sauté the diced pancetta in a large sauté pan over medium-high heat. Spoon the rendered fat out of the pan as it accumulates, always leaving about a tablespoon in the pan. When the pancetta is brown and crisp (after about 5 minutes), add the diced mushrooms and onion. Toss to combine and to coat the mushrooms with the pancetta fat. Cook until the mushrooms are browned, 5 to 6 minutes, stirring once halfway through. When the mushrooms have browned, add the milk. Simmer until the pan is nearly dry, 4 minutes. Remove from the heat.

2. Add the thyme and the lemon juice to the mushroom mixture, tossing to combine. Season with salt and freshly ground black pepper to taste. Top each toast with a layer of the portobello mixture. Serve the bruschetta on a platter while they're still warm.

PANINI OF SMOKED MOZZARELLA, RADICCHIO, AND BALSAMICO

Smoking gives mozzarella a whole different taste and texture, making it tighter, with a distinct smoky aroma. Go for it when you want a little more depth and seriousness than a fresh creamy cheese would offer—for example, with the strong and slightly bitter taste of radicchio. Dried currants are a great way to bring sweetness to the winter produce selections. The smoky aroma of the mozzarella gives this panino a meaty quality, almost like bacon. Adding a drizzle of *balsamico* to the toasted sandwich brightens the flavors.

SERVES 4

4 ciabatta rolls, domed tops sliced off, rolls sliced in half horizontally

6 slices smoked mozzarella, sliced about 1/4 inch thick

1 cup shredded radicchio

4 teaspoons dried currants

Sea salt

Freshly ground black pepper

4 teaspoons *aceto balsamico* (see page 36)

1. Preheat a panini grill to high.

2. Lay the bottom halves of the ciabatta on a clean work surface. Cover each with a single but complete layer of smoked mozzarella. Top each with about 1/4 cup shredded radicchio and a teaspoon of currants. Season with sea salt and freshly ground black pepper.

3. Cover with the top halves of the ciabattas, and grill until the bread is golden brown and the cheese has begun to melt, about 3 minutes. Transfer the sandwiches to a cutting board. Remove the top half of each and drizzle with 1 teaspoon *balsamico*. Replace the tops, cut each sandwich in half, and serve immediately.

APICIAN SPICED CIDER

Named for the Roman gourmet (and glutton) whose name decorates a first-century cookbook, this cider celebrates some of the flavors of southern Asia that were brought to Italy by spice traders. While I don't know if hot apple cider was ever served to Apicius, he surely wouldn't object to this hot-toddy-style drink bearing his name. Skip the Calvados if serving the kids.

SERVES 4 TO 6

1 quart apple cider

1 teaspoon ground allspice

1/2 teaspoon ground cloves

1/2 teaspoon freshly grated nutmeg

Grated zest of 1 orange

1/2 cup Calvados

In a medium saucepan, whisk together the cider, spices, and orange zest. Steep the cider over low heat for 30 minutes, until the cider and the kitchen are aromatic. Strain into a ceramic coffeepot, add the Calvados, and serve steaming hot.

SPIEDINI OF PORK AND FENNEL

Not only is the combination of pork, fennel, and radicchio flavorful and great-looking on the plate, but the use of a dry rub allows for forgiveness in cooking. If the meat is overcooked, the dry rub acts as a flavorful tenderizer. Don't forget to soak bamboo skewers for 10 minutes in water before cooking to prevent them from burning.

Serve the *spiedini* over mixed greens or on a platter with Red Pepper Relish (page 152) alongside.

MAKES 8 SKEWERS

1 teaspoon salt

1 teaspoon sugar

1/2 teaspoon cayenne pepper

1 pound boneless pork loin, cut into 1 1/2-inch cubes

1 large fennel bulb

1 head of radicchio

Extra-virgin olive oil, for drizzling

Sea salt

Freshly ground black pepper

1. Combine the salt, sugar, and cayenne in a small bowl, and mix thoroughly to combine. Dry the pork cubes with paper towels, and then rub them with the spice mixture. Refrigerate the pork for at least 12 hours.

2. Cut the fennel and the radicchio into 1-inch cubes.

3. Thread the skewers, alternating the pork, fennel, and radicchio cubes so that there are 3 of each on each skewer.

4. Preheat a panini grill to high, or preheat the broiler.

5. Grill the *spiedini* for 7 minutes total, turning them once if cooking under the broiler.

6. Drizzle the skewers with the extra-virgin olive oil and season with crunchy sea salt and freshly ground black pepper before serving.

CHEESE PLATE WITH APPLE CONSERVA

Adding a homemade element to store-bought ingredients increases the impact. In this case, cheese is elevated by the accompaniment of apple *conserva*. A sort of adult applesauce, this *conserva* smolders with the low-level heat of black pepper. Serve it in a small bowl on a cheese board for your guests to spoon onto their plates. It cuts the richness of the cheeses and highlights their creamy tang.

The cheese plate should contain a variety of textures, tastes, and types—a hard cow's milk cheese, a soft goat cheese, and a crowd-pleaser, a cheese that almost everyone eats. And then I like to include one of my favorites, La Tur, a creamy blend of cow's, goat's, and sheep's milk.

SERVES 4

FOR THE CONSERVA

4 McIntosh apples, peeled, cored, and cut into chunks

1 tablespoon sugar

1 teaspoon freshly ground black pepper

FOR THE CHEESE PLATE

¾ cup fresh ricotta

6 ounces Rochetta

8 ounces Parmigiano-Reggiano, broken into bite-size pieces

6 ounces La Tur

1. Prepare the *conserva:* Combine the apples and the sugar in a saucepan with a lid. Over a medium-low flame, cook the apples, covered, stirring them every 5 minutes until softened, 15 to 20 minutes. Season with the freshly ground black pepper. (The *conserva* can be stored in an airtight, preferably glass, container for up to 3 days.)

2. Arrange the cheeses on a large platter or board, with the Parmigiano-Reggiano pieces in a pile. Set a bowl of apple *conserva* in the center, and serve.

CHOCOLATE ESPRESSO FONDUE

Nutella, the beloved hazelnut spread, is everyone's favorite dessert panino. This fondue expands its appeal, offering fruit or biscotti instead of bread as the dippers. If you like, add a little Nocce, a hazelnut liqueur. What you dip in chocolate fondue can be as varied as your kitchen pantry. Fruit tastes great, and it can *almost* make this good for you.

SERVES 6

¼ cup Nutella

8 ounces semisweet chocolate chips

8 ounces heavy cream

3 tablespoons brewed espresso

FOR DIPPING

Clementine sections

Cherries

Biscotti

Dried apricots

1. In a fondue pot, combine the Nutella, chocolate chips, heavy cream, and espresso. Over a low flame on the stove, begin melting and combining the ingredients, using a small whisk to blend them.

2. When the fondue is thick and smooth, transfer it to the table, keeping it warm over a Sterno flame at a low setting. Serve with a platter of assorted dippers and enough skewers to go around.

IN FAMIGLIA—
DINNER AT HOME

NOTHING IS MORE SPECIAL THAN TIME WITH FAMILY. THESE SMALL plates build together nicely as a sit-down meal. Choose two or three to combine into a full dinner, or serve the dishes mixed in with favorites from other chapters. The convivial spirit of Italian snacks turns dinner into a relaxed meal filled with delicious options—served family-style, of course.

SHALLOW-FRIED ARTICHOKE HEARTS
WITH LEMON MAYONNAISE

CHILLED TOMATO WATER WITH WARM
MOZZARELLA CROUTONS

PANINI OF GRILLED PORTOBELLOS,
TRUFFLED MAYONNAISE, AND FONTINA

WILTED ESCAROLE WITH MILK-SOAKED
CROUTONS

VEAL INVOLTINI WITH ROASTED GARLIC

WINTER FARRO SALAD

TORTA CAPRESE

SHALLOW-FRIED ARTICHOKE HEARTS WITH LEMON MAYONNAISE

This is a masterful little snack that you can whip up while guests are arriving—a warm little something to hand them along with an aperitif to enjoy while things get under way. Prep the artichoke hearts in advance, keeping them pristine in lemon water. Have your Lemon Mayonnaise ready, and you're in position to serve this luxurious snack with next to no visible labor. And don't be afraid of using a thermometer; it makes your job easier.

SERVES 4

2 lemons, halved

4 artichokes

Approximately 6 cups vegetable oil

1½ cups Wondra flour

Lemon Mayonnaise (page 8)

Sea salt

Lemon wedges, for serving

1. Squeeze the halved lemons into a large bowl of water, and set it aside.

2. Cut off the top half of each artichoke (just below the pointed end) and then cut off the stem end. Discard. Peel off the leaves, starting at the base, leaving only the tender inner leaves that surround the heart. Use a paring knife to trim away all dark spots.

3. Use a spoon to scoop out the thistlelike choke from the center of each artichoke heart. When the hearts are completely clean, place them in the lemon water (where they can be held for up to 2 hours).

4. Heat the vegetable oil in a deep, straight-sided sauté pan over a medium-high flame. The oil should be approximately 2 inches deep.

5. While the oil is heating, pour the Wondra into a shallow bowl. Drain the artichoke hearts, dry them with a paper towel, and cut them into 1-inch cubes. Add the cubes to the bowl of Wondra and lightly dust them.

6. When the oil reaches 370°F, reduce the heat to low. Working in batches, add the flour-dusted artichoke

chunks. Fry for 2 minutes until they are golden. Use a slotted spoon to transfer them to a paper-towel-lined plate to drain while the remaining artichokes are cooked. (Let the oil come back to 370°F before adding the remaining artichokes.) Season with sea salt while the artichokes are still hot.

7. Serve the artichokes with a small bowl of cool homemade Lemon Mayonnaise and fresh lemon wedges alongside.

A candy or deep-frying thermometer will allow you to take the oil's temperature—this guarantees a golden-brown success.

CHILLED TOMATO WATER WITH WARM MOZZARELLA CROUTONS

From the "strictly in summer" category, the clean and pure essence of ripe tomatoes is chilled and served with, well, grilled cheese for grown-ups. The contrast of the cold, refreshing tomato water against the warm cheese toast is fantastic.

Set the tomatoes in the fridge the night before so that you'll enjoy every last drop of their fabulous liquid. This is a dish that reminds us that nature is unpredictable—the amount of liquid given off by eight tomatoes can differ greatly, depending on the fruit. Gauge the amount of olive oil to add by how much tomato water you've got and the depth of its flavor.

SERVES 4

8 large ripe summer tomatoes (heirloom, beefsteak)

1 teaspoon salt

¼ cup fragrant extra-virgin olive oil

4 slices peasant bread, cut 1 inch thick, crusts removed

4 ounces fresh mozzarella, sliced

Sea salt

Freshly ground black pepper

1. Cut the tomatoes in half, then in half again. Season the cut sides with the salt (this draws the moisture from the tomatoes), and place the tomatoes in a large colander set over a large bowl, flesh side down as much as possible. Refrigerate overnight.

2. By morning, the bowl under the colander will have caught the juice that has dripped from the tomatoes. Press the tomatoes against the colander to squeeze forth any remaining juice and throw away the squeezed tomatoes. Swirl the olive oil into the tomato liquid (as you would with salt, taste as you go to gauge the right amount).

3. Toast the bread slices lightly. Cover them with the slices of mozzarella and then toast or top-brown them until the cheese is melted and bubbly. Place a cheese toast in the center of each of four chilled shallow bowls. Divide the chilled tomato water among the bowls, ladling it in around the toasts. Finish with a sprinkling of sea salt and freshly ground black pepper. A chilled spoon makes a nice touch.

PANINI OF GRILLED PORTOBELLOS, TRUFFLED MAYONNAISE, AND FONTINA

Truffled olive oil is pure trickery—olive oil infused with the heady scent of the prized white truffle. It doesn't compare to the real McCoy, but it costs far less and your friends will love the aroma. In this panino, rich homemade mayonnaise is perfumed with truffle oil and partnered with meltingly delicious Italian fontina. Grilled portobellos are the "meat" of the sandwich. This meat-free sandwich is hearty enough for carnivores.

SERVES 4

2 portobello mushroom caps, wiped clean with a damp paper towel

½ cup fresh parsley leaves, roughly chopped

Truffled Mayonnaise (page 8)

4 ciabatta rolls, domed tops sliced off, rolls sliced in half horizontally

4 ounces Italian fontina, thinly sliced

Sea salt

Freshly ground black pepper

1. Preheat a panini grill.

2. Grill the portobello caps (closing the press onto the mushrooms) for 3 minutes. The mushrooms should be slightly charred and softened but still have a firm, fresh feel.

3. When they are cool enough to handle, cut the mushroom caps into a medium dice. In a medium mixing bowl, combine the diced mushrooms, the parsley, and the Truffled Mayonnaise.

4. Spoon the mushroom mixture over the bottom halves of the ciabatta rolls, covering them completely. Lay the sliced fontina over the mushroom mixture in a single but complete layer. Season with salt and pepper before covering with the top halves of the rolls.

5. Grill the sandwiches for 4 minutes, until the bread is golden brown and the cheese has begun to set. Cut each sandwich in half, and serve.

ITALIAN FONTINA A cow's milk cheese from Valle D'Aosta, this is a cheese that was born to melt (thus its starring role in fondue). Seek out the bona fide Italian article.

WILTED ESCAROLE WITH MILK-SOAKED CROUTONS

I'm a big fan of any dish that makes the most of bitter greens. The milk-soaked toasts add richness to humble escarole. It's crisp against wilted, sweet and slightly bitter; in other words, all the great taste sensations are harmoniously balanced. This can be served as a warm salad at the start of a meal or as a side dish with meat. I like the escarole to have just a little crunch left to it. Cook it a few minutes more for a more molten texture.

The ciabatta should soak in the milk for at least an hour or can be made up to 1 day in advance.

SERVES 4

4 tablespoons extra-virgin olive oil

1 head escarole, dark outer tips of the leaves and stem ends removed

1 teaspoon salt

3 garlic cloves, thinly sliced

½ red onion, thinly sliced

Milk-Soaked Croutons (recipe follows)

1. In a large Dutch oven with a tight-fitting lid, heat 3 tablespoons of the olive oil over a medium flame for 2 minutes. Add the escarole leaves, salt, and garlic. Cover, and steam until the leaves are limp, about 5 minutes.

2. Divide the wilted escarole among four small serving plates. Top with the sliced onion, and drizzle with the remaining 1 tablespoon olive oil. Top with the croutons, and serve immediately.

MILK-SOAKED CROUTONS

1 stale ciabatta loaf, cut into 1½-inch cubes

3 cups milk

Olive oil for drizzling

1. Place the bread cubes in a shallow bowl and add milk to cover them. Let the bread soak for 1 hour to absorb the milk.

2. Meanwhile, preheat the oven to 400°F.

3. Drain the bread cubes, squeezing them to remove any excess liquid. Spread the bread cubes in a single layer on a baking sheet, drizzle with olive oil, and toast in the oven, shaking the baking sheet occasionally, until they are gold and crisp, 15 to 17 minutes. If making the croutons in advance, store at room temperature in an airtight container.

VEAL INVOLTINI WITH ROASTED GARLIC

A simple Italian snack that is just as at home on the antipasto table as it is on the dinner table, this makes a quick main course when served with pasta or polenta. Buy good-quality veal (or pork loin) and be vigilant with the cooking time.

SERVES 4

Olive oil

4 cloves garlic, thinly sliced

¼ teaspoon salt

6 slices prosciutto di Parma, cut into thin ribbons

3 cups tightly packed arugula leaves

3 cups Milk-Soaked Croutons (page 59)

⅓ cup milk

1 pound boneless veal loin, cut and pounded into 4 very thin scallops

Sea salt

Black pepper

1. Preheat the oven to 475°F.

2. Heat 1 tablespoon olive oil in a 9-inch sauté pan until it is hot but not smoking. Add the garlic and the salt. Cook, stirring occasionally, until the garlic is translucent, 2 minutes. Add the sliced prosciutto and lightly sauté, 2 minutes. Add 2 cups of the arugula leaves and toss to wilt. Add the Milk-Soaked Croutons, the remaining cup of arugula, and the milk. Combine thoroughly, and remove from the heat.

3. Season the veal scallops on both sides with sea salt and black pepper. Spread the arugula mixture over the scallops and roll them up tightly (starting from the long sides). Skewer along the seam of the meat with metal skewers or bamboo skewers that have been soaked in water for 10 minutes to keep it from unrolling, and lightly coat the outside with olive oil. Transfer the rolls to a parchment-lined baking sheet, and bake for 14 to 15 minutes, until the meat feels slightly firm to the touch.

4. Remove the rolls from the oven and let them rest for 10 minutes before serving. Serve warm, removing the skewers before serving.

WINTER FARRO SALAD

Hands down my favorite grain, farro has an all-day versatility. In the morning, cooked in cream and topped with fresh fruit, it's a different take on oatmeal or granola. For dinner, farro can be cooked in the same fashion as risotto; this is called *farrotto*. Farro, also known as emmer wheat, can be purchased at Italian specialty markets, or wheat berries can be used in its place. (Wheat berries can be found at natural foods stores.)

This is a salad of earthy flavors and textures. Make it at least a few hours in advance so the flavors weave together. A day in advance is even better.

SERVES 4 TO 6

6 cups water

1 cup farro

1 teaspoon salt

½ cup blanched almonds, roughly chopped

Wine-Roasted Garlic (recipe follows)

Seeds of 1 pomegranate (about 1 cup; see page 64)

¼ cup flat-leaf parsley leaves

2 apples, unpeeled, cored and diced (submerge in a bowl of water containing the juice of 1 lemon to prevent discoloration)

6 ounces smoked mozzarella, cut into ½-inch cubes

⅓ cup extra-virgin olive oil

2½ tablespoons balsamic vinegar

Sea salt

Freshly ground black pepper

1. In a medium saucepan, combine the water, farro, and salt. Bring to a boil over a high flame, reduce the heat to a simmer, and cook, uncovered, for 25 minutes, or until tender.

2. Meanwhile, preheat the oven to 250°F.

3. Spread the almonds out on a small baking sheet and toast them in the oven until they are fragrant, 2 to 3 minutes.

4. Drain the farro and spread it on a paper-towel-lined tray to dry, 10 minutes.

5. In a medium mixing bowl, combine the farro, toasted almonds, Wine-Roasted Garlic, pomegranate seeds, parsley, drained apples, and mozzarella. Toss to combine.

6. Whisk the olive oil and the vinegar together in a large bowl. Add the farro mixture, season with sea salt and freshly ground black pepper, and toss well to combine. The salad can be made hours in advance and chilled.

WINE-ROASTED GARLIC

MAKES 1 CUP

20 cloves garlic (2 heads), unpeeled

1 tablespoon honey

Splash of rosé or white wine

1. Preheat the oven to 200°F.

2. Place the garlic cloves on a square of aluminium foil. Drizzle the honey over the garlic, and then add the splash of rosé.

3. Wrap the garlic loosely in the foil and bake for 1 hour, or until the cloves are soft and buttery. Squeeze the garlic out of the peels before serving. If making the garlic in advance, keep the skins on until ready to use.

HOW TO SEED A POMEGRANATE Score the fruit with a knife around its middle, and twist it in half. Hold the fruit above a bowl, flesh side down, and begin rapping on top of it with a soupspoon. The jewel-like seeds, along with their juice, will rain down into the bowl. When the flow of seeds slows, break each half in half again, revealing a new vein of seeds. When the soupspoon method runs dry, use your finger to gently extract the remaining seeds.

TORTA CAPRESE

The best thing about this flourless chocolate cake is that it is crowd-pleasingly delicious, humble on the plate and rich in the mouth, especially with a little fluffy whipped cream alongside. The downside is that it requires two mixing bowls, a food processor, and a springform pan—in other words, more kitchen equipment than I usually like to work with. If you have only one bowl for your mixer, spoon out the chocolate mix, then wash and thoroughly dry the mixing bowl to whip the egg whites—that's how I do it.

SERVES 8 TO 10

Butter and flour for the pan

2 cups whole blanched almonds (12 ounces)

1¼ cups granulated sugar

4 ounces bittersweet chocolate

4 ounces semisweet chocolate

1 cup (2 sticks) unsalted butter

6 large eggs, separated, at room temperature

Confectioners' sugar

1. Preheat the oven to 325°F.

2. Butter and flour a 10-inch springform pan. Fit the bottom with a parchment paper round, and then butter and flour the paper.

3. In a food processor, grind the almonds in 3 batches, adding 2 tablespoons of the granulated sugar each time. Set the almond mixture aside.

4. Combine the chocolates and the butter in a Pyrex bowl or large measuring cup. Melt in a microwave oven on high for 2 to 3 minutes, stirring after each minute, until thoroughly melted and smooth. Set aside.

5. Using an electric mixer with the paddle attachment, beat the egg yolks, gradually adding half of the remaining granulated sugar until the mixture is pale and thick. Add the melted chocolate mixture, beat until incorporated, and then add the almond mixture.

6. Using a wire whisk, beat the egg whites and the remaining granulated sugar until they form stiff peaks. Fold the egg whites into the chocolate mixture in two additions.

7. Pour the batter into the prepared springform pan and bake for 90 minutes, or until a cake tester comes out clean.

8. Cool on a wire rack for 15 minutes before removing the sides of the pan. Dust with confectioners' sugar before serving.

AUTOSTRADA—PICNIC LUNCH

THE ITALIAN ROADWAY REST STOPS OFFER WARM PRESSED SANDWICHES and tidy little bites that inspire these take-along snacks. Along with the umbrella, iced drinks, and sunglasses, eating alfresco is one of the great joys of the summer season. The food is light, tasty, and, most of all, portable. A small folding table becomes an impromptu buffet when draped with a picnic blanket or throw. The already grilled sliced steak panini hold up well during transit. Pack bruschetta toppings and toasts separately, assembling them just before serving for the best-looking picnic buffet. Add cloth napkins, wine, real wineglasses, and music, and your picnic will be complete.

POTATOES WITH 'INO PESTO AND
GREEN BEANS

TIME FOR AN *AMARO*

BRUSCHETTA OF SUMMER SQUASH
WITH RED PEPPER AND MINT

SLICED FLANK STEAK PANINI

BRUSCHETTA OF CELERY, ARUGULA,
AND TOASTED ALMONDS

CHERRY TOMATOES AND BUFFALO
MOZZARELLA SALAD

TWO-BEAN SALAD

EASY ALMOND CAKE

POTATOES WITH 'INO PESTO AND GREEN BEANS

Fresh produce always matters, but never more so than in a salad like this. With so few ingredients in this classic dish, each should be the best available. 'Ino Pesto (which also appears in *Simple Italian Sandwiches*) owes its success to a little softened butter added at the end. It's a staple to keep on hand for sandwiches, pastas, bruschetta toppings, and even as a dip for vegetables.

SERVES 4 TO 6

Sea salt

12 ounces green beans, trimmed and cut in half

3 pounds small new potatoes

1 cup 'Ino Pesto (recipe follows)

Freshly ground black pepper

½ lemon

1. Bring a large pot of water to a boil, adding about 1 tablespoon salt to it. Add the green beans and cook for 4 minutes, or until they are tender but still bright and lively. As they finish, transfer the beans to a colander and rinse under cold water.

2. Add the potatoes to the same pot of boiling water and cook until they are easily pierced with the tip of a knife, 10 to 15 minutes. Drain in a colander and let cool slightly.

3. Combine the beans and the potatoes in a serving bowl. Add the pesto and toss gently to coat the vegetables. Season with sea salt and freshly ground black pepper to taste.

4. Squeeze the lemon half over the salad just before serving.

'INO PESTO

¾ cup extra-virgin olive oil, or more as needed

¼ cup walnuts

2 tablespoons pine nuts

½ garlic clove

¼ teaspoon salt

2 cups tightly packed fresh basil leaves

½ cup freshly grated Parmigiano-Reggiano

1 tablespoon butter, softened

1. In a blender or a food processor, combine the olive oil, walnuts, pine nuts, garlic, and salt. Pulse or blend until smooth. Add the basil in small handfuls, pulsing to combine. When all of the basil has been incorporated, transfer the mixture to a bowl and add the Parmigiano-Reggiano and softened butter, mixing well to combine. The olive oil should form a 1-inch layer above the pesto when it settles. If this is not the case, add more olive oil as necessary.

2. Store, covered, in the refrigerator for up to 3 days. Let come to room temperature before using.

TIME FOR AN *AMARO*

An *amaro*, meaning "bitter," is an after-dinner digestive. There are many types of *amari* made from different herbs and flowers. They are made by monks and families all over Italy, with each region producing a variation on the theme. Whether tasting of anise, citrus, menthol, or mint, this little drink is a world of infinite variations. The right time for an *amaro* is when you've had far too much to eat but plan on having a little bit more. The sweet and bitter taste revives the appetite and, most important, relaxes the stomach. It's something of a miracle.

Restaurants are the best places to sample the many different flavored *amari*. A small tumbler with an ounce or two is the way to drink it. A bottle bought for the home will be on hand for quite a while.

BRUSCHETTA OF SUMMER SQUASH WITH RED PEPPER AND MINT

This is one of the most popular snacks served at my restaurants. When entertaining, I start things off with a cocktail and then I put out a platter of these bright summer bruschetta. The ricotta binds the flavors together for a refreshing little bite—cool and easy. Grill the squash on a panini grill, under the broiler, or on an outdoor barbecue.

SERVES 4

2 medium yellow summer squash

2 medium zucchini

3 tablespoons olive oil

1$\frac{1}{2}$ cups fresh ricotta

6 fresh mint leaves, cut into thin ribbons

Red pepper flakes

Sea salt

Freshly ground black pepper

8 baguette slices, cut $\frac{1}{2}$ inch thick on the diagonal, toasted

$\frac{1}{4}$ cup grated Pecorino Romano

1. Preheat a panini grill.

2. Cut off the stem end of each squash and zucchini. Slice the squash and zucchini lengthwise into $\frac{1}{4}$-inch-thick strips.

3. Lay the squash and zucchini, flesh side down, on the panini grill. Close the top and grill the squash and zucchini for 5 minutes, or until the flesh appears charred. Transfer the squash and zucchini to a cutting board and roughly chop into $\frac{1}{2}$- to $\frac{3}{4}$-inch slices. Transfer the slices to a mixing bowl and add the olive oil, fresh ricotta, and mint leaves. Season with the red pepper flakes, sea salt, and freshly ground black pepper. Toss gently to combine.

4. Divide the squash and zucchini mixture among the toasts, and top each bruschetta with a sprinkling of grated Pecorino Romano.

SLICED FLANK STEAK PANINI

Think of this as an upmarket "cheese steak" with tangy goat cheese and sweet carmelized onions. Well-loved and delicious, this panino is on the most-requested list among friends, families, and customers.

MAKES 4 PANINI

8 ounces fresh goat cheese, preferably Coach Farm

1 tablespoon roughly chopped fresh mint leaves

1 tablespoon roughly chopped fresh basil leaves

1 tablespoon fresh thyme leaves

1½ pounds flank steak

Salt

Pepper

2 Vidalia onions, cut into ½-inch-thick slices

⅓ cup balsamic vinegar

8 slices rustic peasant bread, cut ½ inch thick

1. Using a fork, combine the goat cheese with the mint, basil, and thyme until well blended and smooth. Set aside.

2. Season the steak on both sides with salt and pepper.

3. Heat a sauté pan, preferably cast iron, over a medium-high flame. When the pan is very hot, place the steak in the pan and cook, undisturbed, for 3 minutes on each side, until seared. Transfer the steak to a plate.

4. Add the onions to the sauté pan, and sauté in the rendered beef fat until they are coated, about 1 minute. Season with ¼ teaspoon salt, and then add the vinegar. Cook over a medium flame, stirring occasionally, until the onions are soft and burnished, about 20 minutes. Transfer to a bowl.

5. Preheat a panini grill to its highest setting.

6. Thinly slice the steak, starting at the narrow end.

7. Spread a thin coating of the goat cheese mixture over each piece of bread. Lay the steak slices in a single layer over half of the bread slices, followed by a few onion slices. Top with the remaining slices of bread.

8. Grill the sandwiches until the bread is well browned and the interior is heated through, about 4 minutes. Cut each sandwich in half before serving.

BRUSCHETTA OF CELERY, ARUGULA, AND TOASTED ALMONDS

This bruschetta always looks a little humble at the table, but a platter of them will disappear almost immediately. Crisp, cool, and slightly salty, it's a surprising combination and the best possible use for your underappreciated celery.

SERVES 4

⅔ cup whole blanched almonds

1 teaspoon extra-virgin olive oil

2 cups arugula leaves, loosely packed

3 stalks celery, sliced ½ inch thick on the diagonal

¼ cup 'Ino Mayonnaise (page 8)

Juice of 1 lemon

Sea salt

Freshly ground black pepper

8 baguette slices, cut ½ inch thick on the diagonal, toasted

1. Place a dry pan over a medium flame, add the almonds, and shake the pan frequently until they are toasted, 2 minutes. They should take on light color, give off oil, and become very aromatic. Transfer the almonds to a medium mixing bowl, and when they are cool enough to handle, roughly chop them. Set them aside.

2. Add the olive oil to the same pan and heat it over a medium flame until warm. Add the arugula and toss until it wilts, 2 minutes. Remove the pan from the heat and add the almonds, sliced celery, mayonnaise, and lemon juice. Season with sea salt and freshly ground black pepper, and then fold the ingredients to thoroughly combine. Refrigerate for at least 1 hour or up to 4 hours.

3. Top each toast with approximately 1 tablespoon of the celery mixture, and arrange the bruschetta on a serving platter.

CHERRY TOMATOES AND BUFFALO MOZZARELLA SALAD

This is a variation on the classic Caprese salad using vine-ripened yellow and red cherry tomatoes, which should be bursting with flavor. The traditional basil is mixed with arugula for added depth. This is the time for the best-quality mozzarella that you can find. Mozzarella di bufala, with its tangy taste and creamy texture, would be choice.

SERVES 4

FOR THE VINAIGRETTE

1/4 cup balsamic vinegar

1/2 cup plus 1 tablespoon extra-virgin olive oil

1 tablespoon club soda

1 teaspoon fine sea salt

1/2 teaspoon freshly ground black pepper

FOR THE SALAD

1 cup vine-ripened red cherry tomatoes

1 cup vine-ripened yellow cherry tomatoes

1 cup arugula leaves, loosely packed

1/2 cup fresh basil leaves

2 balls of fresh buffalo mozzarella (about 6 ounces each), drained, cut into 2-inch chunks

Sea salt

Freshly ground black pepper

1. Whisk all the vinaigrette ingredients together.

2. Place the tomatoes, arugula, and fresh basil in a bowl. Toss to combine.

3. Dress the salad with the vinaigrette, and toss again. Divide the salad among four shallow bowls (or place on a serving platter) and then garnish with the fresh mozzarella. Sprinkle with sea salt and freshly ground black pepper.

TWO-BEAN SALAD

This salad is beautiful on a dinner table, colorful when served as part of antipasti, and, yes, it can also be spooned onto toasts as a vibrant bruschetta. This is as versatile as it gets, using indispensable canned beans. And it's good for you, too.

SERVES 4 TO 6

One 16-ounce can white beans, drained and rinsed

One 16-ounce can chickpeas, drained and rinsed

½ red onion, cut into small dice (½ cup)

¼ cup extra-virgin olive oil

1 tablespoon sherry vinegar

2 tablespoons orange juice

2 tablespoons tomato sauce

1 teaspoon salt

1 teaspoon freshly ground black pepper

¼ head of radicchio, cut into thin strips

½ cup thinly sliced red-leaf lettuce (cut into thin strips)

¼ cup fresh basil leaves, chopped

1 tablespoon flat-leaf parsley leaves, chopped

1. About 3 hours before serving, place the white beans, chickpeas, diced onion, olive oil, sherry vinegar, orange juice, tomato sauce, salt, and pepper in a mixing bowl. Toss well to combine, and then set aside at room temperature so that the flavors can permeate the beans.

2. Combine the radicchio, red-leaf lettuce, basil, and parsley in a serving bowl. Add the bean mixture just before serving, and toss to combine.

EASY ALMOND CAKE

In the same way that bread or polenta is your starting point with bruschetta, this simple cake can be dressed in a variety of ways. Sour cherries are a traditional and elegant topping (and specialty stores sell great imported sour cherries in jars). But a scoop of vanilla ice cream and a smattering of toasted sliced almonds do nicely as well. For the sake of simplicity, you can't go wrong with a light dusting of confectioners' sugar and a double espresso. This makes two cakes, one of which can be wrapped and refrigerated for up to 1 week, or frozen for up to 1 month.

MAKES TWO 8-INCH CAKES, 6 TO 8 SERVINGS EACH

1 cup (2 sticks) butter, softened, plus additional for buttering the pans

2 cups all-purpose flour, sifted, plus additional for flouring the pans

1/2 teaspoon salt

1 teaspoon baking soda

1 1/2 cups granulated sugar

7 ounces almond paste

4 egg yolks, at room temperature

1 cup sour cream

1 teaspoon almond extract

Confectioners' sugar, for dusting the cakes

1. Preheat the oven to 325°F.

2. Butter and flour two 8-inch springform pans. Line each with a parchment paper round, and butter the paper.

3. Sift the flour, salt, and baking soda together into a bowl.

4. In a mixer fitted with the paddle attachment, mix the butter and the granulated sugar at medium-high speed until light and fluffy, about 5 minutes. Lower the speed to medium. Break the almond paste into small pieces and add them, a few at a time, beating until smooth, about 8 minutes. Add the egg yolks, one at a time, and then the sour cream and the almond extract.

5. Reduce the mixer speed to low and add the flour mixture in three additions. Mix until just blended.

6. Divide the batter between the prepared pans. Bake for 1 1/4 hours, until the tops are golden brown, the sides have shrunk away from the sides of the pans, and a cake tester comes out clean when inserted into the center of the cake. Cool the pans on wire racks for 15 minutes before removing the sides of the pans.

7. Sift confectioners' sugar on top of the cakes just before serving.

PIZZA

CASUAL AND HANDHELD, PIZZA IS THE ULTIMATE ITALIAN SNACK. One of the most crowd-pleasing things you can serve (grown-ups and children alike go crazy for it), pizza is an opportunity to get creative with your favorite ingredients. The recipes here are a few of my favorite combinations.

BASIC PIZZA DOUGH

PIZZA MARGHERITA

SQUASH BLOSSOM AND RICOTTA
FRESCA PIZZA

BLACK OLIVE, PROSCIUTTO, AND
ARUGULA PIZZA

ITALIAN BEER

PIZZA WITH HEIRLOOM TOMATOES,
SWANKY EXTRA-VIRGIN OLIVE OIL,
AND THE FANCIEST OF SALTS

PEACH, MASCARPONE, AND HONEY
PIZZA

BASIC PIZZA DOUGH The ultimate simple snack, pizza has become a most American form of sustenance. Almost everyone loves pizza, and I'm no exception. There are those who've devoted themselves to defining and duplicating a great crust—armed with noncontact thermometers, water analysis from Naples, and a desire to crack the code. I tend to think more about the toppings: the best mozzarella I can get, the most beautiful tomatoes, an extra-special olive oil.

This is the nonobsessive pizza dough I make at home—kids underfoot, no eye on the clock, and no theories on rise times. And you know what? It's always a hit.

MAKES TWO 12-INCH PIZZAS

1 package active dry yeast

2 cups warm water (about 105°F)

1 tablespoon salt

¼ cup extra-virgin olive oil

4¼ cups all-purpose flour

1. In the bowl of a standing mixer, combine the yeast with the warm water. Add the salt and the olive oil, and stir to combine. Let sit for 5 minutes.

2. Using the paddle attachment, slowly add half of the flour to the yeast mixture. When they are well combined, add the rest of the flour. With the mixer now set to medium (and refitted with a dough hook if you have one), continue mixing until the dough comes together in a smooth ball. Mix for 2 more minutes, until the dough is soft and pliable. Turn it out onto a lightly floured board and knead it gently with your hands for a few minutes.

3. Shape the dough into a ball and place it in an oiled bowl. Cover the bowl with a towel and let the dough rise for 30 to 40 minutes, while you clean

up and prepare your toppings. The risen dough can be wrapped in plastic wrap and refrigerated for up to 2 days or frozen for up to 2 weeks. Defrost overnight in the refrigerator.

4. Turn out the dough onto a floured board, then cut it in half. Press and stretch the dough to form two 12-inch rounds (or two 12 × 6-inch rectangles if you're using cookie sheets rather than pizza pans).

PIZZA MARGHERITA

Famously named for Queen Margherita, this iconic pizza was designed to represent the colors in the Italian flag: red, white, and green. These colors also happen to reflect the seminal Italian ingredients: tomatoes, mozzarella, and basil. Preheat the oven and the pans for at least 30 minutes to get them both to the right temperature.

MAKES TWO 12-INCH PIZZAS

Basic Pizza Dough (page 80)

2 cups Simple Red Sauce (recipe follows)

12 ounces fresh mozzarella, sliced (about 12 slices)

¼ cup extra-virgin olive oil

Sea salt

Freshly ground black pepper

¼ cup loosely packed fresh basil leaves, cut into thin ribbons

1. Preheat the oven and two pizza pans or pizza stones to 450°F.

2. While the pans are preheating, stretch the pizza dough.

3. Carefully transfer the dough to the heated pans. Spread the Simple Red Sauce over the dough, and then arrange the slices of mozzarella over the sauce. Drizzle the olive oil over the pizzas and season with sea salt and freshly ground black pepper.

4. Carefully transfer the heated pans back to the oven and bake until the cheese is melted and bubbly and the crust is crispy, 15 to 18 minutes.

5. Remove the pans from the oven and scatter the basil over the pizzas before slicing and serving.

SIMPLE RED SAUCE

MAKES 2 CUPS

3 tablespoons olive oil, plus 2 additional tablespoons

2 cloves of garlic, peeled and minced

One 28-ounce can whole tomatoes

Salt

Pepper

Heat the olive oil over medium heat. Add the minced garlic and cook until translucent, about 2 minutes. Add the tomatoes and their juice. Using kitchen shears or a knife, cut the whole tomatoes into small pieces. Add salt and pepper and cook until the sauce is thickened and reduced by a third, about 15 minutes, stirring occasionally. Re-season with salt and pepper to taste, and refresh by stirring in a tablespoon or two of olive oil.

GRILLING PIZZA Midsummer heat means that preheating an oven to its upper ranges has next to no appeal. The solution is a backyard pizza on the grill. It takes practice, but the results can be superior to those achieved with a kitchen oven. You'll need to have all of your toppings prepared and at hand. Your grill must be clean and very hot, and you will need tongs. Most important, you will need to get a hot charcoal fire going and to maintain its heat by adding more charcoal if necessary. Lump charcoal, started in a chimney starter, should be added to the side of the fire, not under the main cooking area.

Here's what to do:

After stretching your dough as thin as possible on sheet pans, put it to the side. Holding a ball of paper towel in your tongs, rub oil on your very hot grill. Transfer the stretched dough directly onto the grill and cook for a minute or two. Turn the dough over with the tongs, and then arrange your toppings on the dough. Close the lid on the grill and cook until the crust has bubbled and the cheese has melted. Use a baker's peel to lift the pizza off the grill, or use tongs to pull it onto a serving plate.

SQUASH BLOSSOM AND RICOTTA FRESCA PIZZA

An ethereal combination of fresh flavors, this makes a downright pretty pizza. Squash blossoms, available only in the early summer, are as bright and sunny as a July day. Break out the bubbly and celebrate.

MAKES TWO 12-INCH PIZZAS

Basic Pizza Dough (page 80)

2 cups fresh ricotta

16 fresh squash blossoms

Extra-virgin olive oil

Sea salt

Freshly ground black pepper

1. Preheat the oven and two pizza pans or pizza stones to 450°F.

2. While the pans are preheating, stretch the pizza dough.

3. Carefully transfer the dough to the heated pans. Spread the ricotta over the dough. Arrange the squash blossoms on top, and then drizzle with olive oil. Season liberally with sea salt and freshly ground black pepper.

4. Carefully transfer the heated pans back to the oven and bake until the squash blossoms have crisped at the edges and the cheese is melted and bubbly and the crust crispy, about 10 minutes. Serve immediately.

BLACK OLIVE, PROSCIUTTO, AND ARUGULA PIZZA

I love a pizza topped with arugula not only because it combines the salad portion of a meal with the main course but also because of the peppery bite and leafy texture that it brings to the experience. I scatter black olives over this for a shock of color and for their silky saltiness.

MAKES TWO 12-INCH PIZZAS

Basic Pizza Dough (page 80)

4 ounces fresh buffalo mozzarella, thinly sliced

8 slices prosciutto di Parma

Extra-virgin olive oil

Freshly ground black pepper

1 cup loosely packed baby arugula leaves

1/2 cup pitted black cured olives, such as Gaetas

1. Preheat the oven and two pizza pans or pizza stones to 450°F.

2. While the pans are preheating, stretch the pizza dough.

3. Carefully transfer the dough to the heated pans. Arrange the mozzarella slices over the dough, then follow with the prosciutto slices. Drizzle with olive oil and sprinkle with freshly ground black pepper.

4. Carefully transfer the heated pans back to the oven and bake until the cheese is melted and bubbly and the crust is crisp, 15 to 18 minutes.

5. Remove the pizzas from the oven and immediately scatter the baby arugula and black olives over the top. Drizzle again with a fragrant extra-virgin olive oil, and season with freshly ground black pepper. Slice and serve.

ITALIAN BEER

In the land of Barolos and Chiantis, beer is easily overlooked. Serve a Peroni or a Moretti along with your pizza to give the classic American combination of pizza and beer just a glimmer of a Roman afternoon.

PIZZA WITH HEIRLOOM TOMATOES, SWANKY EXTRA-VIRGIN OLIVE OIL, AND THE FANCIEST OF SALTS

Think of this as a large bruschetta with the freshest of summer tomatoes as a topping. It should be a showcase for the beauty of the season, with yellow, orange, green, and red tomatoes all vying for attention. Only best-quality ingredients need apply.

MAKES TWO 12-INCH PIZZAS

Basic Pizza Dough (page 80)

10 assorted heirloom tomatoes, cored and sliced ¼ inch thick

Sea salt

Freshly ground black pepper

2 teaspoons fresh oregano leaves

¼ cup extra-virgin olive oil

3 ounces Parmigiano-Reggiano, shaved with a vegetable peeler

2 tablespoons pine nuts

1. Preheat the oven and two pizza pans or pizza stones to 450°F.

2. While the pans are preheating, stretch the pizza dough.

3. Carefully transfer the dough to the heated pans. Arrange the tomato slices over the dough, season well with sea salt and freshly ground black pepper, and sprinkle with 1 teaspoon of the fresh oregano. Drizzle with the olive oil.

4. Carefully transfer the hot pans back to the oven and bake until the tomatoes are roasted and slightly shrunken, about 20 minutes. Sprinkle the pizzas with the shaved Parmigiano-Reggiano and cook for 5 minutes more.

5. Sprinkle the pizzas with the remaining 1 teaspoon fresh oregano and the pine nuts. Slice and serve.

SEA SALT Produced in every country with a coast, sea salt is harvested from great salt flats, either by hand or by machine, and then dried in the sun. In an array of colors and textures, the salts from each region have their own distinctive character. There's orange salt from Hawaii, gray salt from Brittany, and the hand-harvested salts of Sicily. The smooth grains and subtle flavor bring out the best in the local fare. Like excellent vinegar, hand-harvested sea salt is a splurge-worthy pantry item, taking a plain tomato to new heights.

PEACH, MASCARPONE, AND HONEY PIZZA

Sweet pizza seems to be a well-kept secret—people are always surprised by it. Italians top their pizzas with pears and Parmigiano-Reggiano, or even figs. For me, the most important aspect of pizza topped with sweet fruit is the black pepper that gives an edge to the sweetness.

MAKES TWO 12-INCH PIZZAS

Basic Pizza Dough (page 80)

8 ounces mascarpone

4 extra-ripe summer peaches, cut into thin wedges

2 tablespoons pine nuts

2 tablespoons raisins

Sea salt

Freshly ground black pepper

¼ cup honey

1. Preheat the oven and two pizza pans or pizza stones to 450°F.

2. While the pans are preheating, stretch the pizza dough.

3. Carefully transfer the dough to the heated pans. Using a rubber spatula, drop the mascarpone in small clumps over the dough. Arrange the peach wedges over the dough, sprinkle with the pine nuts and raisins, and season with sea salt and plenty of freshly ground black pepper.

4. Carefully transfer the hot pans back to the oven and bake until the mascarpone is molten and the peaches appear roasted and slightly shrunken, about 15 minutes.

5. Remove the pizzas from the oven and let them cool for 3 to 4 minutes. Then transfer them to serving platters, and drizzle with the honey. (Use a spoon to dip and drip the honey over the pizza rather than pouring it.) Slice and serve.

BACKYARD BOCCE
TOURNAMENT

SUMMER ENTERTAINING SHOULD BE AS EASY AS OPENING THE DOORS to the backyard. With snacks that evoke the breezes of the Mediterranean, these flavors are salty and fresh, crisp and peppery. Wines should be light and refreshing, with American rosés being a particularly fun choice. These are snacks that leave fingers glistening with olive oil, making bocce ball tossing slightly less precise.

RADISHES WITH BUTTER AND SALT

CHICKPEA AND BLACK OLIVE BRUSCHETTA

SICILIA SUNRISE

JERUSALEM ARTICHOKES WITH ARUGULA AND PINE NUTS

FIG-STUFFED LAMB CHOPS

PANINI OF ITALIAN TUNA WITH RAW FENNEL AND PICKLED RED ONIONS

TRAMEZZINI OF DUCK CONFIT SALAD WITH PICKLED SQUASH MAYONNAISE

RADISHES WITH BUTTER AND SALT

This dish is so simple that it might not warrant a recipe, yet whenever I serve it, people jot down how to prepare it. The focus here is not any one of the three ingredients (though young radishes are most important); the thrill is in the cold, refreshing radishes, the warm butter, and the textural sea salt. This is a convergence of temperatures as much as tastes.

Use young, small radishes (such as icicles or the French breakfast variety) for a flavor that hasn't developed too much pepperyness. Buy them by the bunch (ensuring freshness) and leave a bit of the stem attached for handling.

SERVES 4

2 bunches radishes, leaves trimmed, leaving about 1 inch of stem

½ cup (1 stick) unsalted butter

Best-quality sea salt

1. Rinse the radishes and place them in a colander. Let them drain for a minute or two, and then place them in the freezer if you're going to serve them within 20 minutes, or the back of the refrigerator if you plan to serve them later.

2. Just before serving, melt the butter in a saucepan over medium heat. Pour the melted butter into a small bowl, and fill a small shallow dish with sea salt. Arrange the radishes and the two bowls on a platter or tray.

3. Tell your guests to dip a radish in the butter, and then in the sea salt, and enjoy.

CHICKPEA AND BLACK OLIVE BRUSCHETTA

A great last-minute hors d'oeuvre, this is built from ingredients you probably already have on hand. The strong, salty flavors call out for a cocktail, and the Sicilia Sunrise is a sweet and refreshing solution. Serve the bruschetta with plenty of napkins, as this snack can easily roll down your shirt.

MAKES 8 BRUSCHETTA

One 8-ounce can chickpeas, rinsed and drained

½ cup pitted Gaeta olives, roughly chopped

¼ cup olive oil

1 teaspoon chopped fresh rosemary leaves

Pinch of red pepper flakes

4 ounces ricotta salata, crumbled

Grated zest of ½ lemon

Sea salt

Freshly ground black pepper

8 baguette slices, cut ½ inch thick on the diagonal, toasted

Extra-virgin olive oil

1. Combine the chickpeas, olives, olive oil, chopped rosemary, and red pepper flakes in a sauté pan. Heat over a medium-high flame, stirring frequently, until the chickpeas and olives begin to soften and lose their shape, about 10 minutes.

2. Use a slotted spoon to transfer the chickpea mixture to a bowl. Add the crumbled ricotta salata and the lemon zest. Season with sea salt and freshly ground black pepper.

3. Spoon the chickpea mixture onto the toasts, topping each one with a drizzle of fresh, fragrant extra-virgin olive oil. Don't forget the extra napkins.

SICILIA SUNRISE

This drink is made with Aqua di Cedro, a citron-flavored liqueur (if you can't find Aqua di Cedro, substitute Limoncello). Combine 1½ ounces Aqua di Cedro, ½ ounce vodka, the juice of 2 lemons, 2 crushed mint leaves, and 4 ounces club soda. Shake to combine and serve over ice. Makes 1 drink.

JERUSALEM ARTICHOKES WITH ARUGULA AND PINE NUTS

Not actually artichokes at all, Jerusalem artichokes are a native American plant most closely related to sunflowers (they're also known as "sunchokes"). In the Italian tradition, I serve this earthy ingredient in a rustic salad. The edible tuber is thinly shaved (it has a texture similar to that of a water chestnut) and dressed with a vinaigrette that's enriched with finely grated Parmigiano-Reggiano. It's crunchy, salty, and kind of creamy—in other words, a great way to enjoy this delicious vegetable.

I'll occasionally serve a bowl of this dressing as a dip for crudités.

Slice the Jerusalem artichokes just before serving and toss the slices with a little fresh-squeezed lemon juice to prevent discoloration.

SERVES 4

½ cup pine nuts

½ cup extra-virgin olive oil

1 tablespoon balsamic vinegar

4 tablespoons finely grated Parmigiano-Reggiano

2 cups baby arugula leaves, loosely packed

2 Jerusalem artichokes, peeled and shaved on a mandoline (2 cups), or very thinly sliced

1. Preheat the oven to 300°F.

2. Spread the pine nuts on a baking sheet, and toast them in the oven until they are aromatic, 3 minutes. Remove from the oven and set aside.

3. Combine the olive oil, balsamic vinegar, and grated Parmigiano-Reggiano. Whisk together.

4. In a serving bowl, toss the arugula and the Jerusalem artichoke slices. Add the Parmigiano-Reggiano dressing and toss to combine.

FIG-STUFFED LAMB CHOPS

A substantial "small plate," this double-cut lamb chop is a deluxe and hearty snack. Have your butcher butterfly the chops, then stuff them at home. Your guests will think you went to a lot of trouble—but really, it's hardly any.

SERVES 4

8 double-cut lamb rib chops, 1 bone left in, butterflied to the bone

Salt

Freshly ground black pepper

8 fresh figs or prunes, halved

8 tablespoons (1 stick) butter, cut into tablespoon-size pieces

8 slices prosciutto di Parma

1. Preheat the oven to 450°F.

2. Season the lamb chops on both sides: lightly with salt and liberally with freshly ground black pepper. Stuff each chop with 2 fig halves and 1 tablespoon of the butter. Wrap each stuffed lamb chop snugly with a slice of prosciutto. Place the chops bone down on a baking sheet.

3. Bake for 15 to 17 minutes for medium-rare chops. Serve hot.

PANINI OF ITALIAN TUNA WITH RAW FENNEL AND PICKLED RED ONIONS

Either eat these grilled on a panini press for a crisp and warm sandwich or in their cool and refreshing form. The Pickled Red Onions are mouthwateringly delicious as a sandwich component and are made in advance, so plan accordingly.

MAKES 4 PANINI

One 8-ounce can Italian tuna, packed in oil

Juice of 1 lemon

1 fennel bulb, outer layer removed, cored and cut into a small dice

¼ teaspoon red pepper flakes

4 ciabatta rolls, domed tops sliced off, rolls sliced in half horizontally

1 cup Pickled Red Onions (recipe follows)

Sea salt

Freshly ground black pepper

1. In a medium mixing bowl, combine the tuna, lemon juice, diced fennel, and red pepper flakes. Use a fork to flake the tuna and mix the ingredients. Refrigerate until ready to use.

2. Preheat a panini grill.

3. Spread the tuna mixture over the bottom halves of the rolls. Top each with pickled onion slices. Season with sea salt and some freshly ground pepper and then cover with the tops of the rolls.

4. Grill each sandwich until the bread is lightly golden and crisp, about 3 minutes.

PICKLED RED ONIONS

I use these constantly both at home and in the restaurants. These sweet and sour onions are a favorite garnish. Use a good-quality red wine vinegar.

MAKES 2 CUPS

1 cup red wine vinegar

1 cup water

2 red onions, cut into thin slices

Combine the vinegar and water in a large bowl. Add the onions and cover with plastic wrap. Let sit for at least 12 hours or for up to 2 weeks in the refrigerator. Squeeze excess liquid from the onions before using.

TRAMEZZINI OF DUCK CONFIT SALAD WITH PICKLED SQUASH MAYONNAISE

Tramezzini are delicate by design (crustless sandwiches can't avoid this description), but a hearty filling of duck confit bends the rules. Make the duck salad the day before (along with its Pickled Squash Mayonnaise) and refrigerate overnight to meld the flavors. Then enjoy these very manly tea sandwiches the next day.

Duck confit (pronounced *con*-fee, meaning "preserved") is duck meat that has been braised in rendered duck or goose fat, and then packaged or stored in fat. Neither Italian nor simple, its rich and rustic character nonetheless makes duck confit a delicious addition to the tramezzini tradition. Buy the confit already prepared in specialty stores. If confit doesn't appeal, use duck or chicken breasts, grilled and then diced.

SERVES 4

2 tablespoons pine nuts

2 duck legs confit

¼ cup finely diced red onion

½ head radicchio, thinly sliced

1 cup Pickled Squash Mayonnaise (recipe follows)

8 slices white sandwich bread

4 fresh mint leaves, cut into thin ribbons

1. Preheat the oven to 250°F.

2. Spread the pine nuts on a baking sheet and toast them in the oven for 2 to 3 minutes, until they are lightly colored and aromatic. Remove from the oven and let cool.

3. Heat a dry sauté pan over a medium flame until it is hot. Add the duck legs to the hot pan and cook for 8 minutes, turning them once, to warm the meat and render the fat. When the duck legs are loose and hot, use a slotted spoon or tongs to remove them. When they are cool enough to handle, pull the meat from the bone in bite-size pieces.

4. In a medium mixing bowl, combine the duck meat, red onion, radicchio, and Pickled Squash Mayonnaise. Fold to combine, cover with plastic wrap, and refrigerate for at least 1 hour or, preferably, overnight.

5. To assemble the sandwiches, arrange 4 slices of bread on a clean work surface. Top each with 3 tablespoons of

duck salad and a sprinkling of mint. Top with the remaining slices of bread, and use a chef's knife to remove the crusts. Cut each sandwich in half on the diagonal and serve immediately.

PICKLED SQUASH MAYONNAISE

Gearing the mayonnaise to suit the sandwich is a secret weapon for reinforcing flavor. Here, pickled butternut squash gives homemade mayonnaise a sweet and tart taste. The squash also imbues the mayonnaise with the flavor and color of fall, perfect for heartier sandwiches like duck confit tramezzini. If you don't want to make the mayonnaise from scratch, just add the pickled squash (and some of the pickling liquid it was simmered in) to good-quality store-bought mayonnaise.

Use this on leftover pork loin or chicken breast to transform yesterday's dinner into today's excellent lunch.

MAKES 2 CUPS

FOR THE PICKLED SQUASH

½ cup red wine vinegar

½ cup sugar

½ cup water

1 medium butternut squash, neck only, cut into ½-inch-thick slices (¾ cup of squash)

FOR THE MAYONNAISE

5 large egg yolks

Juice of 1 blood orange or regular orange

½ cup reserved pickling liquid

½ teaspoon salt

¼ teaspoon red pepper flakes

1¾ cups olive oil

1. Prepare the pickled squash up to 2 days in advance: Combine the red wine vinegar, sugar, and water in a medium saucepan. Add the squash slices and bring to a simmer. Cook for 20 minutes, then remove the pan from the heat. Let the squash cool in the liquid, then transfer the slices to a bowl, reserving the pickling liquid.

2. Make the mayonnaise: Combine the egg yolks, orange juice, pickling liquid, salt, and red pepper flakes in a blender, and blend on slow speed.

3. Cover the blender with a lid that has a center opening, or shield it with a towel. With the blender running, drizzle in the olive oil in a slow, steady stream. This should take about 5 minutes. The mayonnaise should begin to thicken amply, at which point a lid is no longer necessary.

4. When all of the oil has been added and the mayonnaise is thick and creamy, transfer it to a mixing bowl and add the pickled squash. Fold to fully incorporate, using a fork to gently break the squash into pieces.

LUNCH BY
THE POOL

GLAMOROUS IMAGES COME TO MIND: BROAD HATS, HOLLYWOOD sunglasses, deep tans. Anything poolside sounds chic, and these snacks are cast with that in mind. Continental flavors built around seasonal American produce make for a fabulous lunch outdoors, even if your poolside costume is not fit for a Roman holiday.

PROSCIUTTO AND MELON WITH
SPICED OLIVE OIL

BLACK OLIVE AND CUCUMBER
TRAMEZZINI

SWEET CORN BRUSCHETTA

FRITTATA OF SUMMER SQUASH AND
PROSCIUTTO COTTO

SHRIMP PANINI WITH PICKLED RED
PEPPERS AND LEMON MAYONNAISE

FAVA BEAN BRUSCHETTA

STUFFED FRIED ZUCCHINI FLOWERS

PROSCIUTTO AND MELON WITH SPICED OLIVE OIL

Sweet melon and salty ham is a classic and familiar pairing. But as with most things, changing one element can make the whole thing seem new—toss a new pillow on a couch, and it brightens the whole room. This classic pairing takes on new life with crispy prosciutto—the saltiness of the ham becomes more pronounced, the sweetness of the melon more refreshing. The spiced olive oil adds a lovely silkiness to it all. A great summer appetizer or salad.

SERVES 4

3 fresh red chiles (serrano, baby red pepper, Jingle Bell)

Extra-virgin olive oil

6 slices prosciutto di Parma

1 cantaloupe, seeded, cut into 1-inch cubes

Fresh baby basil leaves, for garnish

1. Rinse and dry the chiles, and then score each pepper 3 times with a paring knife. Place them in a glass jar, fill the jar with olive oil, and set the jar in direct sunlight for a few hours. (Or if you want to use the oil immediately, warm it over a medium-low flame for 10 minutes.) The spiced olive oil can be stored, covered, in a cool dark place for up to 1 week.

2. Preheat the oven to 300°F.

3. Arrange the prosciutto slices in a single layer on a foil-lined baking sheet. Bake in the oven until the prosciutto has darkened in color and smells like bacon, 6 to 8 minutes. Set aside to cool.

4. When the prosciutto is cool enough to handle, crumble it into bits.

5. Drizzle $1/4$ cup of the spiced olive oil over the melon cubes in a bowl, and toss to coat. (You could chill the melon at this point.) To serve, divide the melon among four plates. Sprinkle each portion with an equal amount of the crumbled prosciutto, and garnish with 2 or 3 fresh basil leaves.

You can make the spiced olive oil a few hours in advance or several days ahead. It will of course take on more heat as the days go by. Use an airtight jar, between 8 and 12 ounces, and a corresponding amount of olive oil.

BLACK OLIVE AND
CUCUMBER TRAMEZZINI

This is a new top-five favorite at 'ino. Based on a traditional tea sandwich, I swapped goat cheese for the usual partner of cucumbers, cream cheese. Black olives add the perfect salty edge.

SERVES 4

2 cups pitted Gaeta olives, roughly chopped

1 cup (8 ounces) Coach Farm goat cheese, at room temperature

8 slices Pullman bread or Arnold Brick Oven White

1 medium cucumber, peeled and cut into $\frac{1}{4}$-inch-thick slices

Sea salt

Freshly ground black pepper

1. Place the chopped olives and the goat cheese in a mixing bowl. Use a rubber spatula to break the goat cheese into smaller chunks, and then fold the two ingredients together to form a chunky mixture.

2. Gently spread the goat cheese–olive mixture over the bread slices. Arrange the cucumber slices over half of the bread—about 5 slices each, to create a single layer with complete coverage. Top the cucumbers with a light sprinkling of sea salt and a few turns of freshly ground black pepper.

3. Close the sandwiches with the remaining 4 slices of bread. Trim off the crusts, and cut each sandwich into 2 triangles.

SWEET CORN BRUSCHETTA

This bruschetta is made with the height of summer's sweet corn—so tender that I don't even cook it. If the corn you're using is a little more mature, blanch the kernels in a pot of boiling salted water for 1 minute.

Fresh ricotta can be added to this for a richer, slightly heftier bruschetta.

MAKES 8 BRUSCHETTA

3 to 4 ears corn (2 cups kernels)

2 teaspoons honey

¼ cup extra-virgin olive oil

¼ teaspoon white wine vinegar

Sea salt

Freshly ground black pepper

Pinch of red pepper flakes

8 baguette slices, cut ½ inch thick on the diagonal, toasted

A few fresh basil leaves, cut into thin ribbons

1. Cut off the pointed end of an ear of corn so it stands flat. Hold it upright in a wide bowl, and use a large chef's knife to cut the kernels away from the cob, from top to bottom, around the whole cob. The bowl will catch the kernels and their liquid. Repeat with the remaining ears.

2. Pour the honey and the olive oil over the corn. Add the white wine vinegar, ½ teaspoon sea salt, freshly ground black pepper to taste, and the red pepper flakes, and toss thoroughly. Set aside at room temperature for 1 hour.

3. Spoon the sweet corn mixture over the toasted bread. Season each bruschetta with a light sprinkling of sea salt and a few turns of freshly ground black pepper. Garnish with the fresh basil, and serve immediately.

FRITTATA OF SUMMER SQUASH AND PROSCIUTTO COTTO

Prosciutto di Parma might be Italy's most famous ham, but prosciutto cotto is the style of ham that most Americans are familiar with. Cooked rather than cured, this prosciutto is moist and meaty—great for sandwiches or for lending its flavor to this simple frittata. Serve the frittata warm or at room temperature. Don't forget to cut it into wedges and put the first slice on a plate for your guests as an inviting little gesture.

SERVES 4 TO 6

2 tablespoons extra-virgin olive oil

3 yellow summer squash, cut in half lengthwise and sliced ½ inch thick

1 overripe medium heirloom tomato, diced

½ teaspoon salt

½ teaspoon black pepper

1⅓ cups ziti, cooked according to package instructions

4 slices of prosciutto cotto, cut into strips

8 extra-large eggs, beaten

½ cup fresh ricotta

1. Preheat the oven to 300°F.

2. Heat a 9-inch nonstick ovenproof pan over a medium-high flame. Add the olive oil and heat until it is hot but not smoking.

3. Add the squash, tomato, salt, and pepper to the hot oil. Toss to combine, and cook until the vegetables have softened, about 3 minutes. Add the pasta and the prosciutto cotto and toss to combine, and heat briefly.

4. Spread the ingredients evenly over the surface of the pan, then add the eggs. As the egg mixture begins to thicken at the edges, use a rubber spatula to pull the edge of the egg mixture toward the center. Jiggle the pan to keep things loose. Continue cooking and pulling the cooked portion of the egg toward the center until the bottom of the frittata is set but the top is still loose.

5. Dot the top of the frittata with the ricotta and then transfer the pan to the preheated oven. Cook for 4 to 5 minutes, until the frittata is set.

6. Remove the pan from the oven and let it cool for 10 minutes. Slide the frittata out of the pan and onto a serving plate, keeping the browned ricotta facing up.

SHRIMP PANINI WITH PICKLED RED PEPPERS AND LEMON MAYONNAISE

For the same reason that lobster rolls are an iconic summer sandwich, this panino is a summer favorite: it is rich and creamy with shrimp and mayo. Pickled Red Peppers and radicchio peeking through give a little sweet and sour crunch. Adding the mayonnaise after grilling is what gives this sandwich its fresh lemony glow—just the thing on a summer afternoon with a glass of rosé. These make terrific hors d'oeuvres if you cut each panino into four finger-sandwich-size strips.

MAKES 4 PANINI

24 medium shrimp, shelled

Sea salt

Freshly ground black pepper

Red pepper flakes

4 ciabatta rolls, domed tops sliced off, rolls sliced in half horizontally

Pickled Red Peppers (page 151), cut into ½-inch strips

1 cup shredded radicchio

Extra-virgin olive oil

¼ cup Lemon Mayonnaise (page 8)

1. Preheat the oven to 350°F.

2. Spread the shrimp on a baking sheet and sprinkle them with sea salt, freshly ground black pepper, and red pepper flakes to taste. Bake for 10 minutes, until the shrimp are opaque. Remove from the oven and let cool.

3. When the shrimp are cool enough to handle, remove the tails and slice each shrimp in half lengthwise, down the back.

4. Preheat a panini grill.

5. Arrange the sliced shrimp in a single layer over the bottom halves of the ciabatta rolls (about 12 shrimp slices per roll). Top the shrimp with the pickled red pepper strips, about 6 per sandwich, and about ¼ cup of the shredded radicchio. Sprinkle with a little sea salt, freshly ground black pepper, and a quick drizzle of olive oil. Cover with the top halves of the rolls, and grill until the bread is golden brown, about 3 minutes.

6. Before serving, remove the top of each sandwich and spread it with 1 tablespoon of the Lemon Mayonnaise. Serve immediately.

FAVA BEAN BRUSCHETTA

Fava beans are a lot of work. There's the outer shell to peel off and then there's the inner skin to peel away—that's a fair amount of surgery for each bright green bean. The payoff for all this prep work is one of the true delights of spring. If the beans are very young and tender, I skip the blanching and go for the raw bean, skin and all (though sensitivities to raw favas are not uncommon). Pecorino Pepato, flavored with whole peppercorns, tops each bruschetta, giving it a finished quality. If you use regular Pecorino, season the bruschetta with coarsely ground pepper.

MAKES 8 BRUSCHETTA

2 pounds fresh fava beans in the shell (2 cups shelled)

Sea salt

3 tablespoons extra-virgin olive oil

Grated zest of 1/2 orange

Pinch of red pepper flakes

1/4 teaspoon freshly ground black pepper

8 baguette slices, cut 1/2 inch thick on the diagonal, toasted

8 shaved slices Pecorino Pepato (about 2 ounces total), broken into pieces

1. Bring a large saucepan of salted water to a boil. While the water is heating, shell the fava beans.

2. Drop the shelled beans into the boiling water and cook for 2 to 4 minutes, depending on the size of the bean, until tender (pull one out, remove the skin, and taste it to determine if it's tender). Drain in a colander and rinse with cold water. When the beans are cool enough to handle, remove the skins in the following manner: Tear off the top of the bean's outer shell and gently squeeze from the bottom. The bean will slide out.

3. Combine the beans with the olive oil, orange zest, red pepper flakes, and freshly ground black pepper in a bowl.

4. Spoon the fava beans over the toasts. Top with the broken slices of Pecorino Pepato and a sprinkling of good crunchy sea salt, and serve.

STUFFED FRIED ZUCCHINI FLOWERS

A fast and fleeting delight of summer, zucchini flowers require TLC: Meander back from the market in the July heat and they might droop before you get home. Keep them on the kitchen counter while you check your e-mail and they could lose their vitality by the time you sign off. While these delicate flowers need to be handled carefully (and kept cool in the refrigerator), they are surprisingly sturdy in a pan of hot oil. Guaranteed to elicit awe in the eyes of your guests, fried zucchini flowers are one of those special snacks that have it all; they're secretly simple to prepare, impress the guests, and are uniquely delicious.

SERVES 8

3 cups fresh ricotta

1 1/2 teaspoons salt

1/2 teaspoon red pepper flakes

1/3 cup olive oil

1/2 cup finely chopped fresh mint leaves

16 zucchini flowers

Vegetable oil, for frying (6 cups)

1 cup Wondra flour

1/2 bottle Prosecco

2 large tomatoes, thinly sliced (8 slices)

Tomato Water (recipe follows)

Coarse sea salt

1. In a mixing bowl, combine the ricotta, salt, red pepper flakes, olive oil, and mint. Mix well to combine. Spoon the mixture into a large self-seal plastic bag, squeeze the mixture toward a lower corner of the bag, and then refrigerate it for at least 30 minutes or overnight.

2. Snip a 1/2-inch hole in the bottom corner of the plastic bag, and pipe the ricotta mixture into each zucchini flower, filling it to the point where the petals begin to separate. Gently twist the petals closed, and set the flower on a baking sheet. When all of the flowers have been filled, refrigerate for 15 minutes.

3. Begin to heat the vegetable oil in a large, deep straight-sided sauté pan over medium heat, monitoring the temperature as it climbs toward 275°F.

4. Whisk the Wondra and the Prosecco together to form a thin, pancake-like batter.

5. When the oil reaches 275°F, dredge a few flowers through the batter to lightly coat them, allowing the excess to drip off. Immediately place the flowers in the pan and

cook for 3 minutes, turning them once, until they are golden brown and appear crisp. Use a slotted spoon to transfer the flowers to a paper-towel-lined tray to drain. Repeat with the remaining flowers, keeping the oil at a steady 275°F.

6. To serve, place a tomato slice in each serving bowl. Drizzle the tomatoes with a few tablespoons of the Tomato Water. Top each with 2 fried zucchini flowers, sprinkle with crunchy sea salt, and serve immediately.

A candy thermometer is recommended to monitor the oil temperature. Make the Tomato Water the night before you plan to serve this.

TOMATO WATER

8 ounces tomatoes, halved

1 tablespoon salt, plus additional for seasoning the dish

Freshly ground black pepper

½ cup extra-virgin olive oil

1 cucumber, seeded and diced

1. Salt the cut side of the tomatoes. Place them, cut side down, in a colander set over a bowl, and refrigerate overnight.

2. Discard the tomatoes, and season the liquid that has dripped from them with salt, freshly ground black pepper, and the olive oil. Add the diced cucumbers. Refrigerate until ready to use.

PROSECCO
PARTY

AS A FORM OF SOCIAL MIXER, THE PROSECCO PARTY IS A WIN-ner. Whether getting to know new coworkers, class parents, or neighbors, an evening of lighthearted snacks and cocktails is an immediate icebreaker. Hors d'oeuvre–style snacks, to be taken with the fingers, are the backdrop for banter and clinking glasses.

GRISSINI WITH FIG PASTE AND PROSCIUTTO

PROSECCO COCKTAIL

PORK SAUSAGE SPIEDINI WITH BOCCONCINI AND CHERRY TOMATOES

BRUSCHETTA ALLA ROMANA

SPIEDINI OF PROSCIUTTO-WRAPPED BOCCONCINI WITH RED PEPPERS

SWEET PEA BRUSCHETTA WITH MINT AND PECORINO

TRAMEZZINI OF LEMON MASCARPONE, SALMON, AND PICKLED ONION

BLOOD ORANGE BELLINI

GRISSINI WITH FIG PASTE AND PROSCIUTTO

The fig butter can be made ahead and refrigerated up to 3 days before using. If fresh figs aren't available, use dried California Mission figs.

MAKES 16 GRISSINI

1 cup (2 sticks) butter, softened

8 ounces fresh figs, stem end removed

16 slices prosciutto di Parma

16 grissini (Italian breadsticks)

1. Combine the butter and the figs in a medium mixing bowl, and stir with a fork until well blended and smooth or pulse in a food processor. (If making in advance, cover with plastic wrap and refrigerate.)

2. Spread a thin layer of fig butter on a slice of prosciutto. Wrap the prosciutto around a breadstick, leaving one end of the breadstick exposed. Repeat with the remaining breadsticks, arranging them on a serving platter as they are completed.

PROSECCO COCKTAIL

Bubbly Prosecco gets a sophisticated edge from two bitter elements: Cynar, made from artichokes, and Aperol, with its bitter orange flavor. These liqueurs add layers of color and nuance to this cocktail. For each drink, combine 4 ounces Prosecco, 1 ounce Cynar, and a splash of Aperol. A small piece of candied ginger is a fun garnish.

PORK SAUSAGE SPIEDINI WITH BOCCONCINI AND CHERRY TOMATOES

Reshape sausage into meatballs and partner it with other adorably round ingredients. These *spiedini* are simple to make and can be eaten by hand, or you can slide the ingredients off the skewers and onto a bed of greens. Bocconcini, or little mouthfuls, are cheerful orbs of mozzarella. Look for them at cheese shops or supermarkets with cheese counters.

Be sure to soak wooden skewers for 10 minutes to prevent burning.

SERVES 6

12 ounces bulk sausage

3 cloves garlic, minced

3 tablespoons minced fresh basil, plus additional for garnish

1 teaspoon salt

½ teaspoon freshly ground black pepper

1 pound bocconcini

12 ounces cherry tomatoes

Fragrant extra-virgin olive oil, for drizzling

1. Preheat the oven to 400°F.

2. In a medium bowl, use a fork to break up the bulk sausage. Add the minced garlic, the 3 tablespoons minced basil, the salt, and the pepper, and blend the ingredients with the fork. Form balls of the sausage mixture, the same size as the cherry tomatoes. (The heat of your hands will soften the fat in the meat and bind the shape.) Place the meatballs on a rimmed baking sheet. Bake until they are brown and have rendered their fat into the baking sheet, 12 minutes.

3. Thread the meatballs, bocconcini, and cherry tomatoes onto 12-inch bamboo skewers, alternating and using 2 of each per skewer. Drizzle olive oil over the skewers and sprinkle with the remaining minced basil.

BRUSCHETTA ALLA ROMANA

This bruschetta is all about anchovies, eggs, and cheese, which means it's hearty, salty, and rich. These should be eaten as soon as they're served. Go for a wine like a Vermentino, which is lush with a great minerality and a racy acidity.

MAKES 8 BRUSCHETTA

2 egg yolks (see note)

4 or 6 teaspoons extra-virgin olive oil (see note)

¼ teaspoon red pepper flakes

3 anchovies

4 tablespoons (½ stick) butter, softened

2 tablespoons fresh lemon juice

8 baguette slices, cut ½ inch thick on the diagonal, toasted

8 ounces best-quality mozzarella, cut into 8 slices

Freshly ground black pepper

1. In a blender, combine the egg yolks, olive oil, red pepper flakes, anchovies, butter, and lemon juice. Puree to a smooth consistency.

2. Arrange the toasts on a baking tray, and top each one with a slice of mozzarella. Under a broiler or in a toaster oven, grill the cheese until it melts and bubbles. Remove the tray from the broiler and transfer the toasts to a serving platter. Spoon the anchovy sauce over each bruschetta, and finish with freshly ground black pepper. Serve immediately.

As in a Caesar salad, the dressing here is built on raw egg yolks—which, for some, constitutes extreme eating. The freshest organic eggs should be used. You can choose not to use raw eggs, and use a total of 6 teaspoons olive oil.

SPIEDINI OF PROSCIUTTO-WRAPPED BOCCONCINI WITH RED PEPPERS

This can be a no-cook cocktail snack, or if you're in the mood to warm them up, a few minutes on a grill changes the character of the bite-size pieces of mozzarella. Similarly, the Pickled Red Peppers can be replaced with an equal amount of roasted red peppers or even crisp, raw red bell peppers. If serving with drinks, cut the skewers in half to make a handheld accompaniment.

You'll need six bamboo skewers—if you're going to grill the *spiedini*, soak the skewers in water for 10 minutes beforehand to prevent burning.

MAKES 6 SKEWERS

9 bocconcini, cut in half

Sea salt

Freshly ground black pepper

9 slices prosciutto di Parma

½ cup Pickled Red Peppers (page 151), cut into 1-inch pieces

Extra-virgin olive oil

6 small squares of focaccia, toasted

1. Lightly season the bocconcini with sea salt and freshly ground black pepper. Wrap each bocconcini half with a half slice of prosciutto.

2. Skewer the prosciutto-wrapped bocconcini and the pieces of pickled pepper, starting and ending with the red pepper (3 bocconcini per skewer).

3. Drizzle each skewer with olive oil. The skewers can be served as is or lightly grilled or broiled, 2 minutes per side.

4. Serve with small squares of toasted focaccia alongside.

SWEET PEA BRUSCHETTA WITH MINT AND PECORINO

Like asparagus, peas announce the arrival of spring, except when you buy the organic frozen ones in midwinter—which, honestly, taste great too. So while the classic pairing of peas and mint is a great warm-weather dish, I serve it year-round.

MAKES 10 BRUSCHETTA

10 ounces shelled fresh peas or frozen organic peas

¼ cup extra-virgin olive oil

½ teaspoon salt

¼ teaspoon pepper

10 baguette slices, cut ½ inch thick on the diagonal, toasted

About 10 fresh mint leaves, cut into ribbons

¼ cup grated Pecorino Romano

1. If you are using fresh peas, blanch them in boiling salted water for 1 minute; drain. If you are using frozen peas, defrost them to room temperature and pat dry.

2. Combine the peas, olive oil, salt, and pepper in a blender. Puree until smooth and bright, about 45 seconds.

3. Spoon about 1 tablespoon of the sweet pea puree onto each of the toasted baguette slices. Top with a few strands of mint and a sprinkling of pecorino.

TRAMEZZINI OF LEMON MASCARPONE, SALMON, AND PICKLED ONION

Taking inspiration from New York's trademark bagels as well as the classic tea sandwich (both are famous salmon and cream cheese vehicles), this tramezzino updates the combination with an uplifting citrus-flavored mascarpone. The main ingredient in tiramisù, mascarpone is a richer, tangier creamy cheese that works well with sweet or savory dishes.

As with all tramezzini, these can be made up to 1 hour ahead and then covered with damp paper towels to retain their freshness.

SERVES 4

$^1/_2$ cup plus 1 tablespoon mascarpone

1 teaspoon lemon zest

1 tablespoon lemon juice

$^1/_4$ teaspoon salt

$^1/_4$ tablespoon freshly ground black pepper

8 slices Pullman bread or Arnold Brick Oven White

4 ounces smoked salmon

$^1/_2$ cup Pickled Red Onions (page 99)

1. Combine the mascarpone, lemon zest, lemon juice, salt, and pepper. Mix with a fork until smooth. (This mixture can be made up to 1 day ahead and kept covered in the refrigerator.)

2. Spread each slice of bread with a thin but complete layer of the lemon-flavored mascarpone. Top half of the bread slices with the smoked salmon and then with pickled onion slices. Top with the remaining slices of bread.

3. To serve, cut the crusts off and slice each sandwich in half diagonally.

BLOOD ORANGE BELLINI

Made famous by Harry's Bar in Venice, the original bellini contains peach purée. In this version, blood orange juice adds a brilliant color to the mix. For each drink, combine 5 ounces Prosecco with 1 ounce blood orange juice. (This is not to be confused with a mimosa, which uses Champagne and its fine sparkling richness. Prosecco is a lighter and infinitely more fun sparkling wine.)

MERENDE—
LATE-AFTERNOON
LUNCH

ITALIANS HAVE AN ENTIRE CATE-GORY DEDICATED TO THE SNACK or small plate; merende is that afternoon snack that is lingered over sometimes until dinner. It's that little salad or wedge of frittata that tides you over till evening. These simple Italian snacks offer a recharge—a time to put down the BlackBerry, pore over the newspaper, and have a civilized bite with a friend.

WARM SHAVED ASPARAGUS SALAD
WITH ANCHOVY DRESSING

RADICCHIO AND CREMINI SALAD

AGRODOLCE SHRIMP AND PEPPERS

SPECK, CABBAGE, AND POPPY-SEED
PANINI

TRAMEZZINI OF VEAL TONNATO
AND ARUGULA

VANILLA ICE CREAM WITH
LIMONCELLO

SALAD OF ARUGULA, PROSCIUTTO,
AND PEACHES WITH PICKLED RED
ONIONS

WARM SHAVED ASPARAGUS SALAD WITH ANCHOVY DRESSING

This dish is a great example of how a slightly different presentation of something familiar can make it seem fresh and new. Cutting asparagus with a vegetable peeler makes for a more textural plate and a crunchier feel in the mouth.

Plus, this dish takes all of 2 minutes to make. It's great for a table of antipasti, as a first course, or to serve as a side dish with fish.

SERVES 4 TO 6

2 bunches asparagus

5 tablespoons extra-virgin olive oil

1 teaspoon anchovy paste

Juice of $\frac{1}{2}$ lemon

$\frac{1}{4}$ teaspoon sea salt

$\frac{1}{4}$ teaspoon freshly ground black pepper

1. Using a vegetable peeler, shave the asparagus stalks (including the tips), creating thin long ribbons.

2. In a small bowl, combine 3 tablespoons of the olive oil, the anchovy paste, and the lemon juice. Whisk to combine. Set aside.

3. Heat the remaining 2 tablespoons olive oil in a sauté pan over medium-high heat until it is hot but not smoking. Add the asparagus ribbons, salt, and pepper, and sauté quickly, tossing with tongs, until the asparagus is warm and slightly curled but still a bright green color, 2 to 3 minutes.

4. Transfer the asparagus to a serving platter. Whisk the dressing again and pour it over the asparagus. Serve immediately.

RADICCHIO AND CREMINI SALAD

Warm salads fulfill a hunger for fresh vegetables and the need on a chilly night for something warm and satisfying. This one, featuring cremini (baby portobello) mushrooms and the mellowed flavor of wilted radicchio, has a bright burst of citrus, always a pleasure. Serve it as a first-course salad or as a side dish to Veal Involtini (page 60).

SERVES 4

3 tablespoons olive oil

1 tablespoon butter, softened

12 ounces cremini mushrooms, including stems, wiped clean with a damp paper towel

Pinch of finely chopped fresh rosemary

Pinch of finely chopped fresh thyme

Sea salt

Freshly ground black pepper

Juice of ½ orange

1 head radicchio, cut into ½-inch-wide strips

1. Heat 1 tablespoon of the olive oil and the butter in a sauté pan over a medium flame until foamy. Add the mushrooms, rosemary, thyme, and salt and pepper to taste. Allow to cook, undisturbed, for 2 minutes, until the mushrooms have softened. Shake the pan to loosen the mushrooms.

2. Add the orange juice to the pan and cook for 2 minutes, until the pan is nearly dry. Add the radicchio and cook until the leaves have wilted, about 1 minute. Fold with tongs to combine. Transfer the salad to four serving plates, and drizzle with the remaining 2 tablespoons olive oil. Sprinkle with some crunchy sea salt and freshly ground black pepper, and serve.

AGRODOLCE SHRIMP
AND PEPPERS

Agrodolce, a mixture of sugar and vinegar, underscores and balances the sweet and sour notes in the ingredients. Shrimp and peppers benefit greatly from this classic Italian flavor combination.

SERVES 4

2 cups white wine vinegar

2 cups sugar

4 red bell peppers, seeds removed, cut into 1-inch-wide strips

$\frac{1}{2}$ teaspoon salt, plus additional for seasoning shrimp

$\frac{1}{4}$ teaspoon red pepper flakes

1 pound medium shrimp (approximately 24 shrimp), shelled and deveined

1 cucumber, peeled, cut in half lengthwise, seeds removed, then cut into $\frac{1}{2}$-inch pieces

1. Combine the vinegar and 1 cup of the sugar in a medium saucepan. Bring to a boil over a medium-high flame. Add the peppers and boil for 5 minutes. Remove the peppers with a slotted spoon, and set them aside.

2. Bring the vinegar-sugar mixture back to a boil. Add the remaining 1 cup sugar and continue to boil until the mixture is reduced by a third, 5 to 7 minutes. Remove from the heat and let cool.

3. Add $\frac{1}{2}$ teaspoon salt and the red pepper flakes to the cooled *agrodolce* mixture. Stir in the shrimp, and refrigerate for 1 hour.

4. Meanwhile, preheat the oven to 400°F.

5. Remove the shrimp from the marinade (reserve the marinade) and place them on a parchment-paper-lined baking sheet. Season the shrimp on both sides with salt. Bake the shrimp for 10 to 12 minutes, until they are firm and opaque. Allow to cool.

6. When the shrimp are cool enough to handle, toss them with the bell peppers and cucumbers in a bowl. Dress with the reduced *agrodolce*. Divide among four plates, or serve family-style from a large bowl or platter.

SPECK, CABBAGE, AND POPPY-SEED PANINI

This panino is built on the traditional flavors of the northern Alto Adige region, where you might sit down to a pasta dressed with these ingredients. *Ubriaco* (or "inebriated") is a cow's milk cheese that's been soaked in the red wine of Lombardy. It's a fabulous cheese, with grape skins pressed into its rind, worth seeking out. Speck, a ham similar to prosciutto, brings all that you expect from a meat that is both delicate and robust.

MAKES 4 PANINI

4 ciabatta rolls, domed tops sliced off, rolls sliced in half horizontally

16 slices speck

1/4 head savoy cabbage, cored, leaves separated

2 teaspoons poppy seeds

1 teaspoon red wine vinegar

4 ounces Ubriaco, thinly sliced

1. Preheat a panini grill to high.

2. Cover the bottom half of each ciabatta roll with 4 slices of speck. Top the speck with a few cabbage leaves, creating a thin but complete layer of cabbage. Sprinkle each sandwich with 1/2 teaspoon of the poppy seeds, and then a drizzle (about 1/4 teaspoon) of the red wine vinegar. Follow with the thinly sliced cheese and then the top halves of the ciabattas.

3. Grill the sandwiches until the bread is golden and crisp and the cheese has just begun to melt.

TRAMEZZINI OF VEAL TONNATO AND ARUGULA

Two things can be said about "veal with tuna mayonnaise." First, it's not an intuitive combination, and second, it's one of the great classic Italian small plates. Somehow it captures the very essence of summer. In the traditional version, pink slices of veal are fanned on a plate and dressed with the lemon-yellow tuna mayonnaise, dotted with capers. It makes your mouth water from the moment it's placed in front of you. I wanted a tramezzini to capture these flavors and created a handheld version of the classic.

SERVES 4

FOR THE TUNA MAYONNAISE (MAKES ½ CUP)

2 teaspoons extra-virgin olive oil

2 tablespoons capers

½ cup 'Ino Mayonnaise (page 8)

Grated zest of 1 lemon

Juice of ½ lemon (2 teaspoons)

⅓ cup canned Italian tuna, drained and broken up with a fork

FOR THE QUICK-ROASTED VEAL

4 veal cutlets, pounded to a ¼- to ½-inch thickness

3 tablespoons extra-virgin olive oil

Sea salt

Freshly ground black pepper

1. Prepare the tuna mayonnaise: Heat the olive oil in a small sauté pan over a medium flame until it is hot but not smoking. Add the capers. They should sizzle when they hit the pan. Shake the pan 1 or 2 times until the capers are fragrant and almost cracking, about 1 minute. Transfer the capers to a paper-towel-lined plate to dry.

2. Combine the mayonnaise, lemon zest, lemon juice, and capers in a bowl. Stir well to combine, and then fold in the tuna. Refrigerate until ready to use.

3. Prepare the veal: Preheat the oven to 400°F.

4. Place the veal on a baking sheet. Rub it with the olive oil and then season it with sea salt and freshly ground black pepper. Roast for 15 minutes. Cool to room temperature.

5. Cut into ½-inch-thick slices.

6. Lay the slices of bread on a clean work surface. Spread each with a thin but complete layer of Tuna Mayonnaise. Divide the veal slices among 4 slices of bread and top the veal with the chopped arugula. Sprinkle with sea salt

FOR THE TRAMEZZINI

8 slices Pullman bread

1 cup arugula leaves,
roughly chopped

Sea salt

Freshly ground black pepper

and freshly ground black pepper before topping with the remaining bread slices.

7. Cut off the crusts and cut each sandwich into triangles.

VANILLA ICE CREAM WITH LIMONCELLO Like an *affogato* (ice cream drowned in espresso), this is a marvelous way to end a meal—a dessert that requires no cooking and really no preparation. The ingredients are probably on hand.

SERVES 4

Vanilla ice cream

Limoncello

1 lemon

4 bowls

Place 1 scoop of ice cream in each bowl. Pour 1 jigger of the Limoncello over each. Using a Microplane, grate a little fresh lemon zest over each, and off you go.

SALAD OF ARUGULA, PROSCIUTTO, AND PEACHES WITH PICKLED RED ONIONS

Use fresh luxuriant peaches for their great sweetness and unparalleled texture in this great summer salad. The Pickled Red Onions have to be made at least 12 hours in advance, and, if they're cold from the refrigerator, add a refreshing surprise to the otherwise room-temperature salad. If there's no time to pickle the onions, use half of a red onion, thinly sliced, instead.

SERVES 4

2 tablespoons red wine vinegar

5 tablespoons extra-virgin olive oil

Sea salt

Freshly ground black pepper

6 cups loosely packed arugula (about 5 ounces)

1 cup Pickled Red Onions (page 99)

8 slices prosciutto di Parma

2 peaches, cut into wedges

1. Whisk together the red wine vinegar and the olive oil, and add salt and pepper to taste. Set aside.

2. Combine the arugula and the Pickled Red Onions in a mixing bowl. Toss with the olive oil and vinegar dressing.

3. Arrange 2 slices of prosciutto on each of four plates. Top with equal portions of the dressed arugula and onions. Garnish each plate with the peach wedges. Sprinkle each salad with sea salt and freshly ground black pepper before serving.

WORLD CUP
FINAL

LIKE THE AMERICAN SUPER BOWL, THIS WORLD SOCCER CHAMPION-ship is a wildly exciting sports event, uniting fans of the game and culminating in a big TV fest. The following recipes aim to elevate the game-time menu while still staying true to the idea that a bunch of guys (and girls too) will gather in front of the television, eats lots of food, and drink beer. Since the World Cup occurs every four years, look to these snacks during the World Series, the U.S. Open, and various NASCAR races. As with the Super Bowl, the mandate is that the food be plentiful, the television gargantuan, and the volume way too loud.

MONTASIO FRICO

VONGOLE

SHALLOW-FRIED SOFT-SHELL CRABS
WITH CAPER MAYONNAISE AND
CITRUS SALAD

BRUSCHETTA OF PICKLED RED PEPPERS
WITH PECORINO PEPATO

PANINI OF OVEN-ROASTED TURKEY
WITH RED PEPPER RELISH AND GRANA
PADANO

COLD PANINI OF FRESH MOZZARELLA
AND PICKLED RED PEPPERS
WITH ARUGULA

MONTASIO FRICO

These melted cheese crisps add a little flourish to a salad or a lacy crispness to fresh fruit. I prefer the oven method over stovetop frying for making larger batches with more consistent results.

Montasio is a Friulian cow's milk cheese with a pleasant melting personality. The cheese is most famous for these golden brown crackerlike snacks.

MAKES 12 FRICOS

1 cup finely grated Montasio

¼ teaspoon finely ground black pepper

1. Preheat the oven to 400°F.

2. Combine the grated Montasio and the pepper in a small bowl.

3. On a parchment-paper-lined baking sheet, sprinkle the grated cheese in 3-inch rounds, using about 3 teaspoons of cheese per frico. Space the fricos about 1 inch apart.

4. Bake until melted and golden, 4 to 5 minutes (overbaking will cause the fricos to turn bitter). Remove from the oven and let cool for 1 minute before peeling the fricos from the parchment paper, using a spatula to loosen the edges. Transfer to a platter, or store in an airtight container at room temperature for up to 2 days.

VONGOLE

Taking roughly 10 minutes to prepare, clams steamed open in a spicy broth look like trouble but aren't. The broth evaporates to steam open the clams and infuses them with flavor. That same broth gets cooked down to a more concentrated sauce, perfect to be soaked up with a hunk of bread.

Serve the clams in big bowls, with the liquid spooned over and toasted bread on the side.

This preparation works equally well with mussels. And yes, you can ladle the steamed clams over their favorite partner, linguine.

SERVES 4

1 cup tomato puree

1½ cups dry red wine

1 tablespoon olive oil

5 cloves garlic, crushed

¼ teaspoon red pepper flakes

2 pounds clams (Mohogany, Littlenecks), rinsed and scrubbed

1 handful flat-leaf parsley leaves, roughly chopped

12 baguette slices, toasted

1. Combine the tomato puree, red wine, olive oil, garlic, and red pepper flakes in a Dutch oven with a tight-fitting lid. Bring to a boil over a medium-high flame.

2. Add the clams and cover the pot. Cook until all of the clams have opened, approximately 3 minutes, discarding those that don't open. Use a slotted spoon to transfer the clams to serving bowls.

3. Raise the flame to high and bring the cooking liquid to a strong boil. Reduce the liquid by half (about 5 minutes), and then spoon the sauce over the clams. Dress each bowl with a sprinkling of chopped parsley and 3 toast slices. Serve immediately.

BUYING CLAMS Purchase the clams on the day you intend to eat them. Keep them in the fridge, in a large bowl covered with a damp towel. They should be alive: tightly closed, or if slightly open, springing closed when touched. Discard any uncooked clams that remain open or that have cracked shells. Rinse them well under cold running water before cooking. The number of clams per pound will vary depending on the size and type, but plan on 4 to 6 clams per person for an appetizer portion.

SHALLOW-FRIED SOFT-SHELL CRABS WITH CAPER MAYONNAISE AND CITRUS SALAD

Soft-shell crabs arrive in the spring and can still be found into summer. For those who love them, they are something to look forward to, and for most, something to be fried. My at-home method of shallow frying offers a crisp crust with less oil. As always, a candy or deep-frying thermometer gauges the temperature of the oil, allowing for good hot frying.

SERVES 4

1 cup Frascati or pinot grigio

2 cups Wondra flour

1 teaspoon salt

½ teaspoon red pepper flakes

6 cups vegetable oil

8 soft-shell crabs, cleaned by your fishmonger

2 cups arugula leaves, loosely packed

1 orange, peeled and separated into segments

1 lime, cut into 8 wedges

Sea salt

Freshly ground black pepper

Caper Mayonnaise (recipe follows)

1. In a large bowl, whisk the wine, flour, salt, and red pepper flakes together to form a batter.

2. Heat the oil in a large, straight-sided sauté pan over a medium-high flame to 375°F.

3. Pat the crabs dry with paper towels. Dip one in the batter, let the excess drip off, and then place it in the hot oil (use a long-handled slotted spoon). Fry the crabs, in pairs, for 3 to 5 minutes per side, or until golden brown. Transfer the crabs to a paper-towel-lined plate to drain. Bring the oil back up to 375°F before adding the next pair of crabs.

4. Toss the arugula leaves and the orange segments together. Spread on a serving platter. Arrange lime wedges around the edge of the platter.

5. Serve the crabs over the salad, sprinkling the platter with sea salt followed by several turns of a pepper mill. Finish with the Caper Mayonnaise spooned over the center of each crab.

CAPER MAYONNAISE

MAKES 2 CUPS

2 cups 'Ino Mayonnaise (page 8)

$\frac{1}{2}$ cup capers

1 tablespoon red wine vinegar

Combine the mayonnaise, capers, and red wine vinegar in a bowl. Blend until smooth. Keep covered in the refrigerator for up to 1 week.

BRUSCHETTA OF PICKLED RED PEPPERS WITH PECORINO PEPATO

Pickled peppers are a great ingredient to have on hand; they can be used in all kinds of ways (in salads, on a cheese board), but they're excellent in sandwiches or in this simple bruschetta. The sweet and sour peppers can be made up to 1 week in advance and kept refrigerated in the vinegar they were simmered in.

SERVES 4

Pickled Red Peppers (recipe follows)

8 baguette slices, cut ¾ inch thick on the diagonal, toasted

4 ounces Pecorino Pepato, thinly sliced, then broken into pieces

Sea salt

Freshly ground black pepper

1. Use a slotted spoon to remove the Pickled Red Peppers from the vinegar mixture. Spread the peppers over the toasts, creating an even layer from crust to crust.

2. Sprinkle each toast with the Pecorino Pepato pieces. Follow with a light sprinkling of sea salt and just a little freshly ground black pepper.

PICKLED RED PEPPERS

These peppers are meant to be softer and more yielding than raw peppers—but not much more. Add them to sandwiches for both their bright flavor and their refreshing bite. Add one to a Bloody Mary to surprise your friends.

MAKES 2 CUPS

3 cups red wine vinegar

1 cup sugar

2 red bell peppers, stemmed, seeded, and cut into 2-inch-wide strips

1. Combine the red wine vinegar and the sugar in a medium saucepan. Stir until the sugar is completely dissolved. Add the red pepper strips, place over a medium-high flame, and bring to a boil.

2. After the liquid begins to boil, remove the pan from the heat and cover it with a tight-fitting lid. Let stand at room temperature for 30 minutes.

3. Store the peppers in enough of their liquid to cover. Store in the refrigerator for up to 1 week.

PANINI OF OVEN-ROASTED TURKEY WITH RED PEPPER RELISH AND GRANA PADANO

Roast the turkey breast in the morning and you'll have afternoon lunch all sewn up. Make the Red Pepper Relish the day before and you can feed a crowd at the drop of a hat. The instructions below are for four panini, but the Oven-Roasted Turkey can easily make eight to ten panini; double the recipe below if preparing for a group.

SERVES 4

4 ciabatta rolls, domed tops sliced off, rolls sliced in half horizontally

¾ cup Red Pepper Relish (recipe follows)

8 ounces Oven-Roasted Turkey (recipe follows), sliced

6 ounces Grana Padano, thinly sliced

1. Preheat a panini grill to high.

2. Spread the bottom halves of the ciabatta rolls with Red Pepper Relish (about 3 tablespoons each). Divide the sliced turkey among the four sandwiches, creating a single but complete layer. Top the turkey with the sliced cheese, again creating a thin but complete layer. Cover with the top halves of the rolls.

3. Grill the sandwiches (place the cheese side up on the grill) until the bread is golden and the cheese has begun to melt, about 4 minutes.

4. Cut the sandwiches in half and serve them hot off the grill.

RED PEPPER RELISH

4 small hot red peppers (bottled), chopped

3 tablespoons extra-virgin olive oil

1 tablespoon red wine vinegar

½ teaspoon salt

½ teaspoon red pepper flakes

Combine all the ingredients in a small bowl and mix thoroughly to combine (you can also pulse them in a mini food processor). This will keep for up to 5 days, covered, in the refrigerator. Bring to room temperature before using.

OVEN-ROASTED TURKEY

1 turkey breast (4 to 5 pounds), preferably brined (see page 154)

4 tablespoons ($\frac{1}{2}$ stick) butter, softened

Salt

Pepper

1 tablespoon fresh thyme leaves

3 tablespoons water

1. Preheat the oven to 425°F.

2. Rinse the turkey breast and pat it dry with a paper towel. Rub 2 tablespoons of the softened butter on the skin of the turkey breast, and then sprinkle it generously with salt, pepper, and the thyme leaves. Place the turkey breast on a rack in a roasting pan. Add the water and the remaining 2 tablespoons butter to the pan.

3. Roast the turkey for 15 minutes. Then reduce the oven temperature to 325°F and continue to roast for $1\frac{1}{2}$ hours, basting every 15 minutes or so. If the skin begins to get too brown, cover the breast with aluminum foil. Roast until the turkey reaches an internal temperature of 160°F.

4. Remove the turkey from the oven and let it stand for at least 15 minutes before slicing.

BRINING Brining, in my experience, is one of the best ways to ensure a juicy bird. A turkey breast, so easily over-roasted to a tight dryness, especially benefits from this small extra step. Use a large glass mixing bowl, or a stockpot lined with a plastic roasting bag, for a 4- to 5-pound breast.

4 quarts water

1 cup kosher salt

2 bay leaves

6 black peppercorns

4 garlic cloves, crushed

1. Combine all the brine ingredients in a stainless-steel pot. Bring to a boil and cook until the salt has dissolved. Let cool to room temperature, and then transfer to a large glass mixing bowl or a plastic-lined stockpot.

2. Rinse the turkey breast under cold running water and submerge it in the brine. Brine the breast for 24 hours, turning it once if it isn't fully submerged. Remove from the brine, rinse briefly, and proceed with roasting.

COLD PANINI OF FRESH MOZZARELLA AND PICKLED RED PEPPERS WITH ARUGULA

This sandwich highlights the fresh and creamy texture of mozzarella. Buy the best mozzarella and bread that you can find, and resist the urge to grill the sandwich. Your reward will be a peerless fresh cheese experience. Top-quality salt and olive oil are also a must.

SERVES 4

4 ciabatta rolls, domed tops sliced off, rolls sliced in half horizontally

8 ounces fresh mozzarella, thinly sliced

Pickled Red Peppers (page 151)

1 cup fresh arugula leaves

Sea salt

Freshly ground black pepper

Extra-virgin olive oil, for drizzling

Arrange the bottom halves of the ciabatta rolls on a clean work surface. Place mozzarella slices on each one for a thin but complete coverage. Spread 2 tablespoons of the Pickled Red Peppers over each sandwich, and then top with a light covering of arugula. Season with sea salt, freshly ground black pepper, and a drizzle of olive oil. Cover with the tops of the ciabatta rolls. (The sandwiches can be wrapped in parchment paper and then foil to be taken along and enjoyed as an on-the-road snack.)

ANTIPASTI

THE QUINTESSENTIAL ITALIAN
SNACK FEST, ANTIPASTI CAN BE
as simple as a few cheeses, some sliced meats, a
handful of olives, and bread. The casual ele-
gance of an antipasto selection should seem almost like an accident, as though it were the
easiest thing in the world to set out an array of
savory snacks for friends who just dropped in,
or for family before the main meal begins. The
more antipasto tables you prepare, the more
practiced you will become. Your repertoire becomes established, and you become known for
those rice balls or those fried olives. Serve a
broad array or a few carefully curated items.
Antipasti are personal and should always reflect the style of the host.

ORANGE-SCENTED OLIVES

SUPPLI

PANINI OF BUFFALO MOZZARELLA
AND ALMOND-HERB PESTO

HARD-BOILED EGGS WITH ANCHOVY
DRESSING

SALAD OF ENDIVE, CURRANTS, AND
SABA

BALSAMIC-GLAZED CIPOLLINE

ROASTED BEET GREEN GRATIN

ROSEMARY PINE NUT SHORTBREADS

ORANGE-SCENTED OLIVES

Embellish olives just a little and they seem a world more special. Here they are warmed with the aromatic skins of oranges. The oil in the skin imbues the olives with a citrus scent, a hint of sweetness, and a splash of fabulous color.

MAKES 1 QUART

2 oranges

1 cup olive oil

Pinch of red pepper flakes

1 quart assorted olives, mixed or your favorite type

1 tablespoon fresh oregano leaves

1. Use a sharp knife to peel the skin away from the oranges, from top to bottom, in wide swaths, leaving as much of the pith behind as possible. Snack on the oranges and put the strips of skin into a small saucepan. Combine the olive oil and the red pepper flakes. Pour into the saucepan and press the skins down to submerge.

2. Heat the oil and the skins over a low flame until warm, about 3 minutes (test with your finger—the oil should be almost hot). Remove from the heat, cover the pot, and let the skins steep in the oil for 10 minutes.

3. Add the olives and half the oregano leaves, stir gently, and replace the lid. Serve the olives that day, garnishing with the remaining oregano leaves, or store them, covered, in the refrigerator for up to 5 days. Bring to room temperature or warm gently over a low flame before serving.

SUPPLI (RICE BALLS)

From the Italian snack hall of fame, rice balls are traditionally made with leftover risotto. I find that there's never any leftover risotto, so I make a dedicated batch the day before. The risotto rests in the refrigerator overnight, making it easy to handle when forming the rice balls. Make sure your risotto is well seasoned with salt and pepper, as that will be the foundation of seasoning for the rice balls.

SERVES 4 TO 6

½ cup polenta or yellow cornmeal

1 cup all-purpose flour

2 eggs

3 cups Basic Risotto (recipe follows), chilled

½ cup finely chopped fresh parsley

4 ounces Italian fontina, cut into cubes

6 cups vegetable oil

Coarse sea salt

1. Combine the polenta and the flour in a shallow bowl. Lightly beat the eggs in another shallow bowl. Set both bowls aside.

2. Combine the chilled risotto and the parsley in a bowl, stirring them together with a fork. Using your hands, form the risotto mixture into golf-ball-size balls. Poke a hole into each rice ball and insert a cube of fontina into it, then close the rice around the cheese. As you form them, set the rice balls on a tray lined with parchment.

3. Pour the oil into a Dutch oven (the oil should be about 3 inches deep), and heat it over a medium-high flame to 360°F.

4. While the oil is heating, dip each rice ball first into the beaten egg, and then into the polenta mixture. Return them to the parchment-lined tray.

5. When the oil has reached 375°F, use a slotted spoon to lower 3 or 4 rice balls into the pot. Cook, turning them occasionally, until they are golden brown on all sides, 4 minutes. Use the slotted spoon to transfer them to a clean paper-towel-lined tray to cool and drain. While they're still hot, season the rice balls with crunchy sea salt. Repeat with the remaining rice balls, maintaining the oil temperature at 375°F.

Risotto is an opportunity to personalize your cooking—add what you love in complementary quantities and combinations. The easiest approach is to cook and season your additions separately, adding them to the rice at the end to heat them: shellfish, such as shrimp or lobster; vegetables, such as asparagus, wilted radicchio, or zucchini; or mushrooms of the season offer a variety of ways to present this well-loved dish. Make sure all of your add-ins are cut to approximately the same size, and go for a balance of flavors and textures.

BASIC RISOTTO

This recipe is a master plan—a blank slate of risotto. It will serve 2 after you hold 3 cups aside for the rice balls.

MAKES 6 CUPS

7 cups liquid (half water, half wine, or all chicken or vegetable stock)

¼ cup extra-virgin olive oil

2 cups diced onions

Salt

Pepper

¼ cup water

2 cups Arborio rice

2 tablespoons unsalted butter

1¼ cups grated Parmigiano-Reggiano

1. In a medium saucepan, heat the liquid over a medium flame. Keep it warm but don't allow it to simmer.

2. In a large Dutch oven, heat the olive oil over a medium-high flame until it is hot but not smoking. Add the onions, salt, and pepper, and cook, stirring occasionally, until the onions are translucent, about 8 minutes. Add the water to the pot and continue cooking the onions until the pot is almost dry, about 4 minutes. Add the rice and stir to combine with the onions and to lightly toast the grains in the hot oil, about 2 minutes.

3. Begin adding the hot liquid, 1 cup at a time, to the rice. Stir in each addition, allowing it to be nearly absorbed before adding the next cup. The heat under the risotto should be high enough to cause the stock to gently

simmer. When all of the liquid has been added and absorbed, taste the rice. It should be creamy and tender. If it isn't, add more liquid. This process may take as long as 45 minutes.

4. Add the butter to the risotto and then gradually add the grated Parmigiano-Reggiano, stirring to incorporate it.

5. If you plan to make rice balls, spread 3 cups of the risotto on a tray and allow it to cool to room temperature. Then refrigerate it overnight.

Vegetable oil is able to take the high heat of deep-frying without breaking down. "Greasy" food is the result of a low frying temperature. A crust should form around the rice balls to prevent the oil from permeating the rice. This happens at 360°F. Use a candy or deep-frying thermometer to maintain the correct temperature.

PANINI OF BUFFALO MOZZARELLA AND ALMOND-HERB PESTO

When you crave fresh flavors in the middle of winter, this usually does the trick. The Almond-Herb Pesto provides a bright accent of citrus against the silky buffalo mozzarella. This is a great plan-ahead sandwich: Make the pesto and the oven-roasted tomatoes the day before, and present fresh and magnificent sandwiches minutes after you hear the words "I'm hungry."

MAKES 6 PANINI

FOR THE ALMOND-HERB PESTO

1 cup plus 3 tablespoons extra-virgin olive oil, plus more if needed

1 garlic clove

Zest of 3 large oranges (scant ½ cup), grated on a Microplane

2 tablespoons fresh orange juice

½ teaspoon salt

2 cups flat-leaf parsley leaves

2 tablespoons fresh thyme leaves

½ cup Parmigiano-Reggiano

1½ cups Marcona almonds, roughly chopped

3 tablespoons butter, softened

1. Prepare the Almond-Herb Pesto: In a blender or a food processor, combine the olive oil, garlic, orange zest, orange juice, and salt. Pulse or blend until smooth. Add the parsley and thyme in small handfuls and pulse to combine. When all of the herbs have been incorporated, transfer the mixture to a bowl and add the Parmigiano-Reggiano, almonds, and softened butter, mixing well to combine. The olive oil should form a 1-inch layer above the pesto when it settles. If this is not the case, add more olive oil as necessary. Store, covered, in the refrigerator for up to 3 days. Bring to room temperature before using.

2. Prepare the Oven-Roasted Tomatoes: Preheat the oven to 275°F.

3. Spread the tomatoes on a parchment-lined baking sheet. Season them with the salt and then drizzle with 2 tablespoons of the balsamic vinegar. Bake for 20 minutes, then drizzle the remaining 2 tablespoons balsamic vinegar over the tomatoes and bake for 20 minutes more. The tomatoes should appear concentrated but still retain a shade of their fresh texture. The tomatoes can be covered and refrigerated for up to 3 days.

2 Roma tomatoes, thinly sliced

¼ teaspoon salt

¼ cup balsamic vinegar

TO MAKE THE PANINI

4 ciabatta rolls, domed tops
sliced off, rolls sliced in
half horizontally

8 ounces buffalo mozzarella

4. When you are ready to make the panini, preheat a panini grill to high.

5. Spread a thin layer of pesto on both the top and bottom halves of the rolls. Arrange the buffalo mozzarella in a thin but complete layer over the bottom halves. Top the mozzarella with 4 slices of oven-roasted tomatoes and then 2 tablespoons of the pesto. Cover with the top halves of the rolls.

6. Grill the sandwiches until the bread is browned and the interior is warmed, 3 minutes.

HARD-BOILED EGGS WITH ANCHOVY DRESSING

The world's most perfect food, hard-boiled eggs are simplicity itself; everyone can cook them, they are almost always on hand, and they are utterly satisfying. Add to that a kicky anchovy dressing and a few slices of bread, and you've got a dish that is disarmingly basic yet sophisticated.

SERVES 6

7 eggs

1/2 cup olive oil

1/2 red bell pepper, seeded and diced

1/2 yellow bell pepper, seeded and diced

2 garlic cloves, smashed

3 anchovies, packed in oil

2 tablespoons roughly chopped flat-leaf parsley leaves

Sea salt

Freshly ground black pepper

1. Cook the eggs (see page 7 for an alternate method): Place the eggs in a large pot of water, set it over medium heat, and bring to a boil. When the water begins to boil, remove the pot from the heat and let the eggs sit, undisturbed, in the hot water for 8 minutes.

2. Remove the eggs from the water, peel them, and slice them into rounds with an egg slicer or a sharp knife. Arrange the slices on a platter.

3. Make the dressing: Heat the olive oil in a sauté pan until it is hot but not smoking. Add the diced peppers, garlic, and anchovies. Gently heat the oil, infusing it with the flavors, for 7 to 10 minutes. Remove the pan from the heat, discard the garlic cloves, and add the parsley leaves. Stir well.

4. Pour the dressing over the egg slices. Finish with a generous sprinkling of sea salt and freshly ground black pepper.

SALAD OF ENDIVE, CURRANTS, AND SABA

Think of saba as a coulda-been balsamic vinegar. The must of the treb-biano grape (that's the juice and the pulp but not the skins) is cooked down to a syrup. If this syrup was aged in the traditional way, it would become balsamic vinegar. As it is, saba is lighter and sweeter than balsamic. Just the thing with the pleasantly bitter bite of endive and the tang of goat cheese.

SERVES 4

¾ cup pine nuts

3 heads Belgian endive, halved lengthwise and cut across into ½-inch-wide strips

2 cups lightly packed arugula

1 cup currants

½ cup extra-virgin olive oil

¼ cup saba

1 tablespoon club soda

Salt

Pepper

One 8-ounce log of fresh goat cheese, cut into 12 slices

1. Preheat the oven to 250°F. Spread the pine nuts on a baking sheet and toast them in the oven until they are lightly colored and fragrant, about 3 minutes (they can burn quickly; if they begin to blacken, discard and start again). Remove from the oven and let cool.

2. Combine the pine nuts, endive, arugula, and currants in a mixing bowl.

3. Whisk together the olive oil, saba, and club soda. Season with salt and pepper. Dress the salad and toss to lightly coat the ingredients. Divide among four shallow bowls.

4. Top each salad with 3 slices of goat cheese and an additional dribble of saba before serving.

BALSAMIC-GLAZED CIPOLLINE

Serve these as part of an antipasto—they're delicious with sliced meats or alongside a cool, crisp salad. For sit-down dinners, they're excellent with roasted meats (particularly pork). They even make a regular appearance on my Thanksgiving table.

MAKES 4 CUPS

2½ pounds cipolline onions (or pearl onions)

2 tablespoons butter

2 tablespoons olive oil

1 cup balsamic vinegar

½ cup water

1. Bring a large pot of water to a boil. Meanwhile, cut an "X" into the root end of each onion. Drop the onions into the boiling water and cook for 2 minutes, then transfer them to a colander.

2. When the onions are cool enough to handle, peel them.

3. In a large straight-sided sauté pan over a medium-high flame, heat the butter and the olive oil until hot. Add the onions and lightly brown them, about 10 minutes. Add the balsamic vinegar and the water, and cook, stirring occasionally, until the onions are tender, 15 to 20 minutes. Use a slotted spoon to transfer the onions to a bowl.

4. Simmer the cooking liquid over a high flame until about ½ cup remains, about 15 minutes. Pour this over the onions.

5. Serve warm or at room temperature.

ROASTED BEET GREEN GRATIN

Ah, the praises of beet greens, carrot tops, and fennel fronds—sung by many who insist that all that greenery be kept, used, and even celebrated. Well, here's one way to use the deeply flavorful and, yes, healthy leaves that are attached to your deeply flavorful and healthy beets. Use the vegetables for Red Beet Salad with Pistachios (page 31) and then keep the greens in the crisper drawer to make this earthy gratin.

The greens get slow-roasted and then tossed with cheese to become a gratin. The slow-roasting takes two hours and can be done the day before.

SERVES 4 TO 6

2 bunches beet tops

¼ cup water, plus more if needed

¼ cup olive oil

1 tablespoon sea salt

Freshly ground black pepper

½ cup finely grated Parmigiano-Reggiano

½ cup fresh ricotta

1. Preheat the oven to 200°F.

2. Spread the beet greens on a rimmed baking sheet. Pour the water over them, and then the olive oil. Season the greens with the sea salt and 1 teaspoon freshly ground black pepper. Toss with your hands to moisten the leaves.

3. Slow-roast the beet greens for 2 hours, tossing them with tongs every 30 minutes. If the pan gets dry, add a few tablespoons of water to keep it moist. The volume of the beet greens will decrease by more than half. They will be limp, dark, and moist when they're done. (The greens can be roasted up to a day in advance and refrigerated until you're ready to make the gratin.)

4. Preheat the oven to 400°F. If you have a separate broiler, preheat it too.

5. Place the roasted beet greens in a 12-inch oval gratin dish. Add the grated Parmigiano-Reggiano and season with 3 turns of a pepper mill. Toss to combine. Dot the top of the gratin with the ricotta. Bake for 10 minutes to thoroughly heat the ingredients.

6. Finish the gratin under the broiler until it browns and bubbles, about 1 minute. Serve hot.

ROSEMARY PINE NUT SHORTBREADS

Shortbread can take on any number of personalities. This one, flavored with two of the big tastes of Tuscany, is comfortable with either tea or wine, and a few put out after a meal are always appreciated. The cookies can be baked, cut, and then frozen in plastic wrap for a few weeks. Otherwise, store the cookies in an airtight tin with a sprig or two of rosemary to make them even more aromatic. This recipe can be doubled and baked in two batches.

MAKES 16 COOKIES

¼ cup pine nuts

8 tablespoons (1 stick) unsalted butter, cut into chunks

½ cup confectioners' sugar

1 tablespoon chopped fresh rosemary leaves

¼ teaspoon sea salt

1 cup all-purpose flour

1. Preheat the oven to 350°F.

2. Spread the pine nuts on a foil-lined cookie sheet and lightly toast them in the oven for 3 minutes. (Pine nuts burn easily. If they begin to brown, discard and start again.) Set the nuts aside to cool.

3. Melt the butter in a medium saucepan over medium heat. Remove the pan from the heat and stir in the confectioners' sugar, rosemary, pine nuts, and salt. Stir in the flour to form a dough.

4. Use your fingers to spread the dough into an ungreased 8-inch square baking pan. Bake until lightly golden and firm, 20 minutes.

5. Cool the pan on a baking rack for 2 minutes, and then use a sharp knife to cut into 16 squares. Let the cookies cool completely in the pan before removing them with a small offset spatula.

ACKNOWLEDGMENTS

My most sincere thanks to all the great people I work with at 'ino, 'ino-tecca, Lupa, and Bar Milano, who allow me to step away and work on projects like this (and pick up my kids from school). Micah Shapiro, who's taken care of 'ino like it was his own; Mark Cantu and Liz Carr, who've helped keep Lupa the vital and vibrant place that it is; and Ethan Richardson, who somehow manages to get it all done all the time. And a special thanks to Steve Conaughton for his inherent dedication and integrity.

I'd also like to thank the team of people who helped put this book together: my collaborators and friends, coauthor Kathryn Kellinger and photographer Mike Piazza; the always supportive Vicky Bijur and Ed Levine; and, of course, Peggy Hageman and David Sweeney for having faith in another one. Thanks to all.

—Jason Denton

Cheers to Peggy Hageman at HarperCollins for keeping us on track and almost on time—her willingness to step into various roles (including hand model and recipe taster) has made our job easier and even more fun. Peggy, along with David Sweeney, has been a delight to work with and we've enjoyed every minute of it.

Hats off to Vicky Bijur, agent extraordinaire, for all her attention and encouragement and insight.

A shout-out to Michael Piazza for his talent, generosity, and, dare I say it, flexibility. Thank you for never saying no to yet another drive south on the Mass Pike. A double high five to my coauthor and captain of this ship, Jason Denton: As always, your energy and zeal are contagious, your knowledge is inspiring, and your impromptu dinners are awesome. I am indeed lucky to work alongside you on this and other important pursuits like badminton and tie-dye. I'm thrilled to count you and Jennifer among my nearest and dearest, as it makes the big city feel like the best version of a small town.

And finally, a little kiss for Lee Hanson. Thanks for absolutely everything.

—Kathryn Kellinger